Happy Cooking!

Stephanie + Jeff

$18.87
ISBN 978-0-87197-594-2
51887>

9 780871 975942

Two Million Meals Later

House Recipes from Boise's Brick Oven Bistro

Manufactured by

Favorite Recipes® Press

An imprint of

P. O. Box 305142
Nashville Tennessee 37230
1-800-358-0560

Two Million Meals Later

House Recipes from Boise's Brick Oven Bistro

Stephanie Telesco and Jeff Nee

Illustrations by Jennifer Proffitt

InDesign and Production Consultant
Wendi Navarro, Lumen Creative
wendi@lumen-creative.net

Southwestern Publishing Group

There is no love sincerer than the love of food. George Bernard Shaw (1856-1950)

Dedication

Our deep thanks to every one of you who created and shared the soul of the Brick Oven Bistro. Steph & Jeff

The pleasures of the table are of all times, and all ages, of every country and every day. Jean-Anthelme Brillat-Savarin (1755-1826)

Food is the first enjoyment of life. Lin Yutang (1895-1976)

Let's Do Lunch!

*The S's   Salads, Sandwiches, Soups and
Stews! Pages 7 - 148*

Meet you for Supper! What's for Dinner?

*Hot Open Faced Sandwiches and Dinners
and, yes, Corny Pots! Pages 149 - 171*

Today's Special!

*If it's Monday, it must be Red Beans & Rice
and more! Pages 172 - 224*

Eat Dessert First!

Cookies, Bread Pudding and Shakes! Pages 225 - 252

A Note From the Illustrator

The most important element of the Brick Oven Bistro to me was the feeling of home. I wanted to capture the warmth and the tradition that I felt. I worked at the Brick Oven Bistro for four years while attending Boise State University and I have never felt more at home in a place I worked. I really did love my co-workers, my guests, and of course the food.

I chose to use linocuts printed by hand as the basis for the illustrations. They too carry a sense of tradition and elegance. They feel like home. Each one is very labor intensive, but the results are unmatched by any other media out there. The cover is a hand colored linotype. I used watercolor just as thousands of printmakers have done before me. This book was a labor of love for me and I hope it shows. Should you wish to see more of my artwork or commission me for a project please visit my online portfolio and blog at www.jenniferproffitt.blogspot.com.

With Love,
Jennifer "Lara" Proffitt

 # Let's Do Lunch!

Bread is the warmest, kindest of words. Write it always with a capital letter, like your name. Russian Proverb

Our Bread came to us from Rich's company as frozen dough. Then twice, if not more a day, we would pull it, thaw it, cut it, roll it, proof it and bake it! Bread was the common denominator, everyone rolled bread. We had contests to learn who could do it the best – that meant great looking and fast!

And to the tune of the TV show Rawhide, some staff will remember - "Rollin, rollin, rollin, keep this bread a rollin, Beanerie......!"

Rich's does not sell its bread in grocery stores. There are "white" breads in the stores, that one could use for our sandwiches, but for our Sunflower Seed Cracked Wheat Bread, we have not found a bread that we would use.

In our quest for bread, we called Stacie Applegate-Wells, a woman who worked for us when she was in college and delightfully returned to work for us in our last year and helped us close the restaurant. She has been a much appreciated member of our Bistro family! Stacie is a graduate of BSU Culinary School, now the CWI Culinary School, and an experienced bread baker. She bakes bread for her family and her grateful friends and gifted Jeff and I, on more than one occasion, with her delicious results.

Stacie was up to the task and within days, she had developed, tested and finalized these recipes. We are so grateful to her for accepting the challenge and creating these recipes!

Stacie's Sunflower Seed Cracked Wheat Bread

2 Cups Bread Flour
2 TBSP Yeast
¼ Cup Honey
¼ Cup Canola Oil
2 tsp Table Salt

1 Cup boiling Water
½ Cup Cracked Wheat

1 ½ Cups Whole Wheat Flour
2 Cups Bread Flour

½ Cup toasted Sunflower Seeds

Mix the 2 Cups of Bread Flour, Yeast, Honey, Canola Oil and Table Salt together and leave it to sit for an hour.

Place the Cracked Wheat in the boiling Water, mix well and let it sit for 20 minutes.

After an hour, Add 1 ½ Cups of Whole Wheat Flour and 2 Cups of Bread Flour and using a dough hook, process for at least 5 minutes. Add Sunflower seeds and mix until incorporated.

Place in an oiled bowl to rise, cover with a cloth towel and leave for about an hour to an hour and a half or until it has doubled in size.

Deflate the dough and once again cover with a cloth towel and leave for about an hour to an hour and a half, or until it has doubled in size.

Deflate the dough, divide it into 4 equal pieces and roll each into a 12 inch roll.

Place the rolls on a baking sheet lined with parchment paper, and cover with a cloth towel until double in size, then bake at 400 degrees for 11-15 minutes.

As the bread comes out of the oven, brush it with Bistro Egg Wash.

Bistro Egg Wash

1 Egg
2 TBSP Water
¼ tsp Roasted Garlic Powder
¼ tsp Thyme

Whisk together and brush on the baked bread!

Clearly there will be those of you who love making bread, so Stacie also created this Italian bread. This way, you have the option to make it at home!

Stacie's Italian Bread

2 Cups Bread Flour
2 TBSP Yeast
¼ Cup Honey
¼ Cup Canola Oil
2 tsp Table Salt

4 Cups Bread Flour

Mix 2 Cups of Bread Flour, Yeast, Honey, Canola Oil and Table Salt together and leave it to sit for an hour.

After the hour, add 3 Cups of Bread Flour, using a dough hook, and process for at least 5 minutes.

Place in an oiled bowl to rise, cover with a cloth towel and leave for about an hour and a half or until it has doubled in size.

Deflate the dough, cover with a cloth towel and leave for about an hour to an hour and a half, or until it has doubled in size.

Deflate, divide it into 4 pieces and roll each into a 12 inch roll. Place the rolls on a baking sheet lined with parchment paper, and cover with a cloth towel until double in size, then bake at 400 degrees for 11-15 minutes.

As the bread comes out of the oven, brush it with Bistro Egg Wash.

Now that we have the Bread for you, let's move onto Sandwiches.

"Too few people understand a good sandwich." James Beard

As the folks who worked for us will confirm, we had reasons for everything that we did. Whether it was rolling bread, greeting guests, offering meal suggestions, or making Sandwiches, we had clear ideas on best practices! If you have ever had a deli sandwich that has been in a cooler all day, you will appreciate what follows.

Bistro Sandwich Philosophy

Think about difference in temperatures and textures. In anything, it is what makes flat become full. Apply this to a sandwich and what you have is: The bread is warm and soft, the dressing is cold and creamy, the tomatoes, cold and soft, the shirred Romaine cold and crunchy and the meat warm and tender. We believed in layers, one leading into the other and always the idea of creating a perfect sandwich!

"Beef Because the West Wasn't Won on Salad!"

Iowa Beef Industry Council

Hand-carving our Meats

Clearly our choice to hand carve our meats increased our staff training. However, the difference between our meat and meat sliced by a machine was significant enough to us to continue the way of the "Luddites". David Sax, author of Save the Deli , wrote in the Atlantic, in 2009 about the reasons for slicing meat by hand. He writes about the lead slicer, Beni, at Katz's Deli in New York, and says: "The [meat at Katz's] is so good because when you slice by hand the juice stays in the meat," Beni told me that night. When you put pastrami on a slicing machine, it is pressed against the blade, and the precious moisture, which makes the difference between a dry sandwich and a succulent one, often ends up dripping on the counter." If you have a chance, try it yourself.

Our Meats

Our meats were always chosen with taste and quality as the criteria. We are very grateful to all our purveyors who were our partners in our quest for quality. For Turkey, we developed a product with Foster Farms. For Bacon, Daily's out of Montana was our choice. For Beef and Pork we used Snake River Farms Double R Ranch and Kurobuta products. For Ham, we chose Farmland Original Pit Ham and our Chickens were fresh and hand cut.

Our Sandwiches

BLTC - Mayonnaise, Sliced Tomato, Marinated English Cucumber, Shirred Romaine, Bacon.

Breast of Turkey - Mayonnaise, Sliced Tomato, Marinated English Cucumber, Shirred Romaine, Turkey.

Bistro Club - Mayonnaise, Sliced Tomato, Marinated English Cucumber, Shirred Romaine, Turkey, Bacon.

Bistro Muffuletta - Horseradish Mayonnaise, Sliced Tomato, Cheese, Shirred Romaine, choice of Meat, Muffuletta mix.

Sirloin of Beef - Horseradish Mayonnaise, Sliced Tomato, Marinated English Cucumber, Shirred Romaine, Beef.

French Dip – Horseradish Mayonnaise, Beef, Au Jus Sauce.

Yankee Pot Roast - Horseradish Mayonnaise, Sliced Tomato, Marinated English Cucumber, Shirred Romaine, Pot Roast.

Sugar Cured Ham – Cherried Mustard, Sliced Tomato, Marinated English Cucumber, Shirred Romaine, Ham.

Reuben Hamwich – Horseradish Mayonnaise, Cheese, Ham, Creamy Kraut.

Carolina Chicken - Mayonnaise, Sliced Tomato, Marinated English Cucumber, Shirred Romaine, Diced Sweet Gherkins, Carolina Chicken.

Texas BBQ Pork – Sliced Tomatoes, Sliced Bistro Pickles, Pulled Sauced Kurobuta Pork, Bistro BBQ Sauce.

Bistro Veggie – Cherried Mustard, Horseradish Mayonnaise, Sliced Tomato, Marinated English Cucumber, Cheese, Sliced Hard Boiled Egg, Shirred Romaine, Muffuletta mix.

Chicken or Turkey Cranberry - Mayonnaise, Sliced Tomato, Marinated English Cucumber, Shirred Romaine, Chicken or Turkey, Cranberry Relish.

Chicken or Turkey Caesar Salad - Mayonnaise, Sliced Tomato, Marinated English Cucumber, Shirred Romaine, Chicken or Turkey Caesar Salad.

Chicken or Turkey Parmesan – Pepper Parmesan Dressing, Sliced Tomato, Marinated English Cucumber, Shirred Romaine, Chicken or Turkey.

Chicken or Turkey Tarragon Salad- Mayonnaise, Sliced Tomato, Marinated English Cucumber, Shirred Romaine, Chicken or Turkey Tarragon Salad.

Cashew Chicken or Turkey Salad - Mayonnaise, Sliced Tomato, Marinated English Cucumber, Shirred Romaine, Cashew Chicken or Turkey Salad.

Chicken or Turkey Slawich - Mayonnaise, Sliced Tomato, Marinated English Cucumber, Shirred Romaine, Chicken or Turkey, Creamy Coleslaw.

Chicken or Turkey Cordon Blu - Ranch Dressing, Sliced Tomato, Marinated English Cucumber, Cheese Shirred Romaine, Ham and Chicken or Turkey.

Bistro Creole Egg Salad - Mayonnaise, Sliced Tomato, Marinated English Cucumber, Shirred Romaine, Gaucho Beef mix.

Bistro Cheesesteak – Beef dipped in au jus sauce, Peppers and Onions, Cheddar Cheese Sauce.

Gaucho Beef - Horseradish Mayonnaise, Marinated English Cucumber, Shirred Romaine, Gaucho Beef mix.

Bistro Picadillo - Marinated English Cucumber, Creamy Coleslaw, Picadillo mix.

Beef, Pork or Ham Peppers and Onions - Horseradish Mayonnaise, Sliced Tomato, Marinated English Cucumber, Cheese, Shirred Romaine, Beef, Pork or Ham, Peppers & Onions.

Beef or Pork Po'Boy - Horseradish Mayonnaise, Sliced Tomato, Marinated English Cucumber, Cheese, Shirred Romaine, Beef or Pork, Burgundy Mushroom Gravy.

San Francisco Beef Salad - Horseradish Mayonnaise, Sliced Tomato, Marinated English Cucumber, Shirred Romaine, San Francisco Beef Salad.

Swedish Meatball - Horseradish Mayonnaise, diced Bistro Pickle, Swedish Sauced Meatballs sliced in half.

Tuscan Meatball - Horseradish Mayonnaise, Sliced Tomato, Marinated English Cucumber, Shirred Romaine, Tuscan sauced Meatballs sliced in half, Parmesan Cheese.

Thai Chili Pork – Marinated English Cucumbers, Creamy Coleslaw, Thai Chili Pork.

Beanery Mayonnaise

The original recipe was for 5 gallons! Several times a week we would make mayonnaise, devising innovative ways to slowly drip the oils into the mixing bowl! With concerns about the safety of eggs, we abandoned homemade mayonnaise, going the route of a commercially produced product. If you are comfortable with the eggs you buy, do try this, as the flavor is wonderful!

2 Eggs (50 – 55 degrees)

2 tsp Kosher Salt
1 tsp White Sugar
¾ tsp Coleman's Mustard

2 ½ Cups Canola Oil (50 – 55 degrees)
1 Cup Olive Oil (50 – 55 degrees)

2 ½ TBSP Apple Cider Vinegar (50 – 55 degrees)
½ tsp Lemon Juice

Beat the Eggs at high mixer speed for 2 minutes.

Add the dry ingredients and beat for 2 more minutes.

Add the Oils in a very slow stream while beating

When all the oil is emulsified add the remaining ingredients.

Scrape down the bowl and beat for one more minute.

Refrigerate until ready to use. This recipe yields 1 Quart.

*From our Bistro mayonnaise, we made our Horseradish Mayonnaise,
the recipe of which follows!*

Horseradish Mayonnaise

Our Horseradish Mayonnaise is a delicious accompaniment to
most any sandwich. We also served this as a condiment with our
Beef, Meatloaf and Pot Roast dinners. It adds a bite that enlivens
taste buds. If you are not making your own mayonnaise, purchase
a good quality mayonnaise to get the best consistency and flavor.

> 2 ½ TBSP Horseradish
> ¾ tsp Salad Mustard
> ½ tsp Lemon juice, fresh squeezed
> ½ tsp Worcestershire Sauce
> ½ tsp Kosher Salt
>
> 1 ½ TBSP Parsley, chopped
>
> ⅓ Cup Sour Cream
> 1 ⅓ Cup Mayonnaise

Add all the ingredients into a bowl and whisk until completely
mixed together.

Yield is 2 Cups

Cherried Mustard

Long before Emeril Lagasse coined "kick it up a notch", we were doing so with this sauce on our Ham sandwiches. There are those of you who were such fans, that a to-go container accompanied you home! And then, there were those who requested, "Without that hot stuff that you put on it!" This is incredibly simple to make - with the right Black Cherry preserves! We spent some time sourcing a readily available product, trying a few, before we found one that works well. It is the Hero Black Cherry Fruit Spread. We found it at Fred Meyers. Best to make this a day ahead of using it, so that the flavors can meld!

> 12 oz Hero Black Cherry Fruit Spread
> ½ Cup + 1 TBSP Salad Mustard
> 3 TBSP Horseradish
> 2 TBSP Soy Sauce

Place all the ingredients in a large bowl.

Whisk until the Cherries are almost smooth, but still a bit chunky.

Yield is 2 ½ Cups

🌱 During Cherry Season consider making your own Cherry fruit spread and freezing or canning it!

Bistro Muffuletta

There are two variations here – the first was our original, which contains Anchovy Paste. The second was our vegetarian variation which uses Soy Sauce and Sesame Oil, and was the one we served for years to honor our vegetarian guests.

This mix is best when it sits for a day or two. We used this on our Muffuletta sandwich and as a topping on our Salads.

Original Recipe:

>1 ¼ Qts Cauliflower, chopped
>
>1 ½ Cups Carrots
>
>¾ Cup Black Olives, sliced
>1 Cup Green Olives, sliced
>
>¼ Cup Parsley, minced
>1 ½ tsp Garlic, minced
>2 ½ tsp Capers, minced
>¼ Cup Red Onions, chopped
>
>2 ¼ tsp Oregano
>1 ½ tsp Sweet Basil
>
>2 TBSP + 1 tsp Anchovy Paste
>1 ½ Cup Olive Oil

Remove the stem from the Cauliflower and set aside. Chop the florets and place them in a large bowl.

Place the Cauliflower stems in a food processor and pulse until small dice. Add to Cauliflower in large bowl.

Place Carrot pieces in a food processor and pulse six times, until small dice. Add to large bowl.

Drain Olives and place in food processor. Pulse twice until small dice. Add to large bowl.

Add Parsley, Garlic, Capers and Onions to large bowl.

Add Oregano and Basil to large bowl and mix well.

In a separate bowl, whisk Anchovy Paste fully into the Olive Oil.

Slowly add the Anchovy Oil to the ingredients in the large bowl, mixing everything thoroughly.   Refrigerate until ready to use.

Yield is 1 ¾ Quarts.

♣ OTHER IDEAS Muffuletta is wonderful combined with vegetables as a side dish, mixed with pasta, as a topping on sliced meats and used in mini quiches which we served as Hors D'oeuvres at our Wine Classes! We believe it is one of great taste delights, and we like to always have some on hand!

Vegetarian Version:

> 1 ¼ Qts Cauliflower, chopped
>
> 1 ½ Cups Carrots
>
> ¾ Cup Black Olives, sliced
> 1 Cup Green Olives, sliced
>
> ¼ Cup Parsley, minced
> 1 ½ tsp Garlic, minced
> 2 ½ tsp Capers, minced
> ¼ Cup Red Onions, chopped
>
> 2 ¼ tsp Oregano
> 1 ½ tsp Sweet Basil
> 2 TBSP Soy Sauce
>
> 1 ½ Cup Olive Oil
> 1 ½ tsp Sesame Oil

Remove the stem from the Cauliflower and set aside. Chop the florets and place them in a large bowl.

Place the Cauliflower stems in a food processor and pulse until small dice. Add to Cauliflower in large bowl.

Place Carrot pieces in a food processor and pulse six times, until small dice. Add to large bowl.

Drain Olives and place in food processor. Pulse twice until small dice. Add to large bowl.

Add Parsley, Garlic, Capers and Onions to large bowl.

Add Oregano and Basil to large bowl and mix well.

In a separate bowl, whisk Soy Sauce and Sesame Oil fully into the Olive Oil.

Slowly add the blended Oil to the ingredients in the large bowl, mixing everything thoroughly. Refrigerate until ready to use.

Yield is 1 ¾ Quarts.

Belker Full Sour Pickle

Over the years we used several different brands of Pickles. Steinfelds, which we used, are readily available in the market. To these crisp pickles, we added a few more items, once again in the interest of improving flavor!

    1 TBSP Jalapeno, chopped
    2 tsp Garlic
    1 tsp Black Peppercorns

    1 46 oz Dill Pickles, full sour

Place the Jalapeno, Garlic and Peppercorns into the jar of Pickles. Cover and refrigerate for 5 days before using.

Marinated English Cucumbers

We like the addition of "crunch" that these add to a sandwich!

    1 Cup White Vinegar
    2 TBSP Soy Sauce
    2 TBSP Granulated Sugar
    2 drops Tabasco

    1 English Cucumber, Sliced

Place the White Vinegar, Soy Sauce, Granulated Sugar and Tabasco in a bowl and whisk until the Sugar has dissolved.

Add the Sliced Cucumbers and marinate for ½ hour. Drain and enjoy!

Bistro Creamy Kraut for Reuben Hamwich

This recipe is an improvement to using plain Kraut for a Reuben. Do try to find a really good Kraut. They are out there, and yes, they are more expensive, however the quality is worth the expenditure! We encourage you to consider a Reuben Turkeywich – substituting Turkey for Ham. It's a taste treat!!

    2 Cups Sauerkraut
    2 TBSP Bistro Pepper Parmesan Dressing

Mix the Sauerkraut with the Pepper Parmesan and heat slightly.

Yield is 2 Cups.

♣ *Shared Memories!*

Hi, I wanted to tell you my story about the Beanery...I never have gotten used to calling it the "Brick Oven Bistro." I am a vegetarian and as such every time I have wanted to order a sandwich have been subjected to every version of "cucumbers and sprouts with cream cheese and tomato" out there. Because of this I loved the Beanery's Muffuletta Sandwich. It was so nice to be able to order something other than the standard vegetarian fare.

When I was at St Luke's in labor with my son, things did not progress as fast as everyone expected, so by late afternoon my husband and mom were discussing what to do for dinner. Not unexpectedly they decided on the Beanery. I of course spoke up and said I wanted my favorite Muffuletta sandwich. "You can't have that, they won't let you eat while you're in labor" they told me. "Get me a sandwich!" I tried to say calmly. I saw them give each other a look that basically told me they were going to humor me and get me a sandwich they never thought I would eat. Hours later, at 10:37, our son was born healthy and handsome. After all of the excitement of the birth died down I realized I was incredibly hungry - 15 hours of labor will do that. I remembered my sandwich and even though it was about 5 hours old, it was the best sandwich I have ever had...and I will remember it forever!

Hilary Dunstan

25

Original Brick Oven Spicy Chicken for Sandwiches

There is some forethought needed for this sandwich. Be sure to cut the chicken breasts so that they are the same thickness. Marinate the chicken at least 24 hours so that it will taste properly. In the restaurant, baked and julienned, the pieces were served with a slice of our bacon, mayonnaise, shirred romaine lettuce and sliced tomato on our freshly baked bread. We used a wonderful chicken breast for this. When the chicken we used for this recipe changed and we could not find a consistently good product, we replaced this sandwich with our Carolina Spicy Chicken.

1 Cup Lime Juice
2 Cups Sprite
1 Qt Water, cold
1 ½ TBSP Worcestershire Sauce
½ tsp Lime Zest
1 TBSP Chili Powder
2 TBSP Cumin
½ tsp Coriander
1 TBSP Oregano
½ tsp Cayenne
½ tsp White Pepper
½ tsp Black Pepper, coarse grind
2 TBSP Kosher Salt

2 Lbs Chicken breasts, cut to a similar thickness

Place all liquid ingredients and spices in a large shallow container. Mix fully, insuring that the Salt is dissolved in the liquid.

Add the Chicken breasts, insuring that they are fully submerged in the marinade. Cover and refrigerate for at least 24 hours and up to 2 full days.

When ready to bake, preheat oven to 300 degrees. Place the Chicken on a sheet pan and bake for 10 – 12 minutes until completely cooked in the center.

Remove from the oven, cover with a piece foil, to retain the heat. After 5 minutes, remove the foil, and julienne the pieces as desired. Yield is 8 - 10 Sandwich portions

♣ *Thoughts about our variations!*

We constantly strove to balance tradition and innovation in our menu. Truth be known, we like variety in our cuisine, so while there were always the tried and true classics, Jeff and I were always searching the marketplace and world for new menu items that fit our culinary vision. We certainly appreciated that you helped us in creating a new generation of comfort food classics!

Carolina Spicy Chicken

1 ¼ Lbs Chicken breast
1 tsp Kosher Salt
1 tsp Black Pepper, coarse grind

5 TBSP Butter
2 ½ TBSP Garlic, minced
2 tsp Chipotle Peppers in Adobo Sauce
1 Cup Orange Juice
¼ Cup Cilantro, chopped

2 tsp Salad Mustard
2 tsp Worcestershire Sauce
2 TBSP Cilantro, chopped
¼ tsp Kosher Salt

Trim the Chicken Breast, cut it in half, separating the fatter end from the thin end. Slice the fatter piece in half down the side, so that all the pieces end up approximately the same thickness.

Season the Chicken with Salt and Pepper and let sit for 20 minutes before cooking.

Melt the butter in a large sauté pan, over medium high heat. Sauté the Garlic and Peppers for 3 minutes.

Place the Chicken in the pan in one layer. Add the Orange Juice and Cilantro. After 3 minutes of cooking time, flip each piece and continue cooking for another 3 minutes.

Remove the chicken from the pan and place in one layer on a sheet pan to cool slightly.

Add the Salad Mustard, the Worcestershire, the Cilantro to the sauté pan and reduce the liquid by half.

Shred the Chicken and return it to the liquid. Mix fully. cook for 1 minute. Taste and add the Salt if needed. Yield is 6 – 8 servings.

Texas BBQ Pork

We used Snake River Farms Kurobuta Pork Shoulder for this sandwich. Lucky us and you! Making this Pork is a two day process. Aficionados know it is well worth your time and effort.

    8 Lbs Pork Shoulder

Pork Shoulder Rub:
1 ½ tsp Paprika
1 ½ TBSP Smoked Hot Paprika
1 TBSP Kosher Salt
1 TBSP Garlic Powder
1 ½ tsp Black Pepper
1 ½ tsp Cayenne Pepper
1 ½ tsp Onion Powder
1 ½ tsp Oregano
1 ½ tsp Thyme
Pork Shoulder Braising Liquid:
1 TBSP Black Peppercorns

1 ½ Cups Dark Beer
1 TBSP Kosher Salt
1 TBSP Thai Bird Chilies or Jalapenos
3 Qts Water

Day One: Wash and dry fully the Pork Shoulder. Place on a small tray.

30

Mix all ingredients for the Pork Shoulder Rub in a small bowl.

Rub this mixture all over the Pork. Cover the Pork with plastic wrap and place in the refrigerator for at least twelve hours.

Day Two: Place Peppercorns in a piece of cheesecloth or a small coffee filter, and tie with a string, long enough so that you can tie this off on one of the handles of a large sauce pot.

Add all the remaining ingredients to the sauce pot.

Place the Pork into the sauce pot. Add additional water if necessary so that the Pork is fully submersed in liquid.

Braise the Pork over a low heat for 2 ½ to 3 hours, to fork tender.

Remove from the Braising liquid, allow to cool slightly until you are able to pull the Pork apart into long strands.

Add 1 Quart of the BBQ Sauce (recipe follows) to the Pork.

Bistro BBQ Sauce

This sauce has many uses. It sauces the Texas BBQ Pork above, and it makes a wonderful sauce for BBQ Chicken.

This BBQ sauce livens up a Beef Sandwich and adds some kick to roasted veggies or a stir-fry!

½ tsp Beef Base
2 TBSP Water, hot

¼ tsp Garlic, minced
¼ Cup Yellow Onion, minced

1 TBSP Brown Sugar
2 TBSP Chili Powder
¼ tsp Liquid Smoke
1 TBSP Cider Vinegar
1 TBSP Salad Mustard
¼ Cup V-8 Juice

1 Qt. BBQ Sauce, Cattleman's preferred

Mix the Beef Base with the hot Water until fully dissolved. Place in a sauce pot.

Place all remaining ingredients into the sauce pot and bring to a boil. Reduce heat and simmer until the onions are fully cooked.

Yield is 1 Quart.

Chicken or Turkey Caesar Salad

Incredibly simple and delicious, this makes a great sandwich as well as a great topping for crisp Greens.

1 Lb Chicken or Turkey, cooked and julienned

¾ Cup Red Onion, chopped
¼ Cup Parmesan Cheese
¾ Cup Bistro Caesar Salad Dressing (Pg 54)

Place all the ingredients in a large bowl and mix gently and well. Yield is 1 ¼ Quarts.

Chicken or Turkey Tarragon Salad

Poultry salads are a delicatessen staple all over this great land of ours. To give ours a slightly more exotic flair, we add tarragon!

1 Lb Chicken or Turkey, cooked and julienned

¼ Cup Yellow Onions, minced
¼ Cup Green Onion, minced
2 TBSP Parsley, minced

Dash Cayenne Pepper
¼ tsp Kosher Salt
¾ tsp Tarragon
½ tsp White Pepper
¾ Cup Mayonnaise

Place all the ingredients in a large bowl and mix gently and well. Yield is 1 Quart.

Cashew Chicken or Turkey Salad Sandwich Mix

We always had the inspiration of having cooked chicken and turkey on hand. And we were always inspired to create new menu items. These two combined in the creating of this sandwich filling, which was loved by many. The next time you have Chicken on your menu, cook more and enjoy this!

¾ Cup Cashews, halves or smaller random pieces

1 ½ Lb Chicken or Turkey, cooked and julienned
⅓ Cup Green Onion, white and green parts, chopped
⅓ Cup Yellow Onion, chopped
1 ½ TBSP Parsley, chopped

1 ⅓ Cup Mayonnaise
¼ tsp Kosher Salt
Dash Cayenne Pepper
¼ tsp White Pepper

Toast the Cashews, either on the stove in a small sauce pan over low heat, or in a 300 degree oven on a baking sheet, until they are slightly browned. Set them aside to cool.

Combine the remaining ingredients in a bowl and mix completely.

Add the toasted Cashews, just as you use this, so that they remain crunchy.
Yield is 2 Cups, enough for 5 or 6 sandwiches.

Bistro Creole Egg Salad

Always in search of a better way to make a dish, this was the result of our efforts when it came to Egg Salad. Try this as well with smoked hard boiled Eggs – Delightful!

12 Eggs, hard boiled, smoked and chopped

1 Cup Celery, minced
¼ Cup Red Onion, minced
¼ Cup Parsley, minced
2 cloves Garlic, minced
1 ½ TBSP Capers, drained and minced

½ tsp Balsamic Vinegar
1 ½ tsp Dijon Mustard
1 ½ tsp Paprika
1 ½ tsp Granulated Sugar

1 Cup Horseradish Mayonnaise

Place all the ingredients in a large bowl and mix carefully. Refrigerate.

Yield is 6 servings.

Cheddar Cheese Sauce for Bistro Cheesesteak

For this sauce, you can use a Cheddar Cheese spread, we found one from Kahunia, or you can grate Sharp Cheddar cheese. Both work well!

1 TBSP Butter

½ tsp Garlic, minced
1 tsp Onion, minced

1 Cups Heavy Cream

6 TBSP Cheddar Cheese Spread or
½ Cup Sharp Cheddar Cheese, grated finely

⅛ tsp Kosher Salt
⅛ tsp White Pepper

Place the butter in a sauce pan and melt.

Add the Garlic and Onion and sauté for 2 minutes, until the garlic begins to change color.

Add the Heavy cream to the saucepan and bring to a boil. Reduce the heat and simmer until the mixture has reduced by half.

Add the Cheese Spread or grated Cheese and stir until fully melted

Add Kosher Salt and White Pepper, taste and adjust seasonings as desired.

Yield is 1 ½ Cups.

Gaucho Beef Salad Sandwich

Watching documentaries on Argentina's Pampas and barbeques of Argentine beef, were the inspiration for this sandwich.

½ Lb Beef, cooked and julienned thinly

¼ Cup Green Pepper, minced
⅔ Cup Yellow Onion, minced
½ Pc Bistro Pickle, minced
2 ½ TBSP Green Olives, sliced
1 TBSP Roasted Red Pepper, minced
1 TBSP Green Chilies, diced

Dressing:
4 ½ tsp Red Wine Vinegar
1 tsp Dijon Mustard
½ tsp Garlic, minced
Dash Tabasco Sauce

¼ Cup Olive Oil

Place Beef, Green Pepper, Yellow Onion, Pickle, Olives, Pepper and Chilies in a bowl and gently mix.

Place the Vinegar, Mustard, Garlic and Tabasco in a separate small bowl and slowly whisk the Olive Oil into this mixture until fully incorporated.

Pour the Dressing over the Beef and other ingredients, mix gently and thoroughly.

Taste and adjust seasonings, adding Kosher Salt and Coarse Black Pepper if desired.　　Chill fully.　Yield is 3 ¼ Cups.

❧Shared Memories!

My husband and I used to go to the original location, where Addies is now, on dates; we have been married almost 30 years. Pretty much every year, to celebrate an event during the rare times that we ever ate out, it was always hands down the Brick Oven Beanery that we chose due to the consistent service and great food!

We have eaten there with a lot of relatives who were visiting from out of town and who are now long gone.

When we heard that you were closing, we ate there as much as we could afford and also I filmed the atmosphere so we would not forget and pinned a napkin up in our office.

So, as you can imagine, it's more than the cookbook...it's memories that are evoked from the very taste of the favorite foods we ate there; after so many years, it's genetic.

Thanks again for all the hard work and the benevolence of producing the cookbook, Debi Carpenter

Bistro Peppers and Onions

We made this with both Green and Red Peppers and enjoyed it on Beef, Ham or Pork sandwiches. It is a good addition to a pasta dish as well.

1 TBSP Olive Oil

1 ½ Cups Green Peppers, julienned
½ Cup Red Peppers, julienned
3 Cups Yellow Onions, sliced thinly

½ tsp Granulated Sugar
½ tsp Kosher Salt
¼ tsp Black Pepper, coarse grind

Heat the Olive Oil in a saucepan.

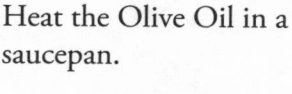

Add all the ingredients into the sauce pan and sauté over medium heat until fully cooked.

Yield is 2 ½ Cups.

Bistro Picadillo

We love foods from all over the world. This was inspired by
Cuban Sandwiches we enjoyed in Miami and San Francisco.

½ Cup Dark Raisins
1 tsp Beef Base
¾ Cup Water

1 TBSP Olive Oil
¾ Cup Yellow Onions, chopped
1 Lb Ground Beef

½ Cup Chili Powder
¾ tsp Cinnamon
1 TBSP Tomato Paste

1 TBSP Balsamic Vinegar
1 14 oz can Diced Tomatoes
1 ½ tsp Sugar

Place the Raisins, the Beef Base and the Water in a small sauce pot,
simmer for 15 minutes. Reserve for use later

Heat the Olive Oil in a sauce pan, add the Yellow Onions, Ground
Beef, and spices and Tomato Paste.
Sauté until the Onions and Beef are tender and cooked.

Add the Balsamic Vinegar, Diced Tomatoes and Sugar and reserved
raisins and simmer for 10 minutes.   Yield is 1 Quart.

On August 28, 2009, in our blog we wrote :

It's not that we don't like burgers... Never mind the t-shirt hanging behind the register with the image of a burger with a slash through it. That's just us being cheeky. You know how we roll at the Brick Oven Bistro.

Truth is, we like a good burger now and then. What red blooded American carnivore doesn't? So when people ask us the question, "if you guys are all about 'comfort food', why don't you serve hamburgers?", we just smile indulgently, point them to the first two words in our tag line ("New Adventures" -- but you knew that)...then we call security and have them ejected (just kidding).

The point is that while a great hamburger fits the "comfort food" bill, you could hardly call it a "new adventure". So why should we put something on our menu that you can get just about anywhere when there are so many more interesting things we can offer you?

Let's take today's special for example: our Beef Peppers & Onions Sandwich. Here's how we do it. We start with thin, hand-carved slices of roast beef (see last week's blog, "Cuts Like a Knife"), pile it on fresh-baked Italian or Sunflower Wheat bread slathered with horseradish mayo, add fresh lettuce, tomato, and cucumber, then top the glorious mess with sauteed onions and red peppers. hoping you'll forgive this slight imperfection. If you want to kick it old school (aka, picnic style), we add some coleslaw and Rum Pot Beans on the side. Now, look us in the eyes and tell us honestly that you'd rather have a cheeseburger. We didn't think so.

San Francisco Beef Salad

This remains one of our personal favorites, which we make over and over again. Often we will double the "Liquid" and have it on hand in the refrigerator so that we can create this on the spur of the moment. The Beef is as good in a sandwich as it is on top of crisp greens. It has been a dinner salad many a happy night!

> The Liquid:
> 4 Pcs Star Anise
> ½ Cup Soy Sauce
> 2 Garlic cloves, minced
> ¼ Cup Brown Sugar
> 6 TBSP Rice Vinegar
>
> The Sauce:
> 1 Cup Mayonnaise
> 2 TBSP Dijon Mustard
> ½ Cup of the "Liquid"
> 1 ½ TBSP Sesame Oil
>
> The Salad:
> 2 Lbs Beef, cooked, thinly sliced and julienned
> 3 Green Onions, thinly sliced on the diagonal

Place all the ingredients for The Liquid in a sauce pot. Bring them to a boil, then reduce the heat and simmer for 5 minutes. Remove from the stove and refrigerate overnight.

The next morning, remove the Star Anise and proceed to make the

Sauce. Place all the ingredients for The Sauce in a bowl and mix thoroughly.

In a separate large bowl, add the julienned Beef and the sliced Green Onions. Pour the Sauce into the bowl and mix thoroughly. Garnish with Sesame Seeds if desired.

Bistro Meatballs

42

This recipe for meatballs is what we used for our Swedish and Tuscan Meatball Sandwich and our Italian Wedding Soup.

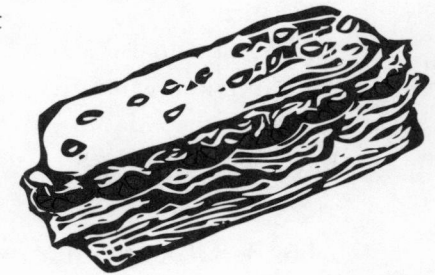

3 slices White Bread, crusts cut off
¾ Cup Milk

½ Lb Ground Beef
½ Lb Ground Pork

1 Egg

3 Garlic cloves, minced
4 TBSP Parsley, minced
1 Cup Parmesan Cheese, grated finely
½ tsp Oregano, Thyme or Dill
½ tsp Kosher Salt
¼ tsp Black Pepper, coarse grind
2 TBSP Canola Oil

Preheat the oven to 325 degrees.

Place the Bread and the Milk in a shallow baking dish. After about 5 minutes, using your hands or a potato masher, mash fully.

Place the mashed Bread in a large bowl.

Add the remaining ingredients and mix well by hand.

Portion into the size you wish. ¼ Cup for the meatball sandwiches, 1 TBSP for the Italian Wedding Soup meatballs.

Place the Canola Oil in a sauce pan and heat over medium high heat until shimmering.

Add the Meatballs and cook until browned on all sides. If you are making the small meatballs for the Italian Wedding Soup, reserve them for use in the recipe.

43

For the Sandwich Meatballs, place the Meatballs in a baking dish and cover with the Sauce of your choice. Bake for 10 minutes.

Yield is 4 – 6 Servings for the Sandwich Meatballs.

❧ Other Ideas : These meatballs are great in a classic Italian Tomato Sauce over Spaghetti. In the Swedish Sauce, they are delicious served over Egg Noodles topped with chopped Dill. In the Tuscan Sauce try them with Perciatelli or substitute an Alfredo Sauce for a delicious alternative. We have had great luck freezing them. What a delight to come home to these for dinner!

Swedish Sauce

2 Cups Burgundy Mushroom Gravy (Pg 162)
¼ tsp Dill
1 TBSP A1 Sauce
¼ Cup Sour Cream

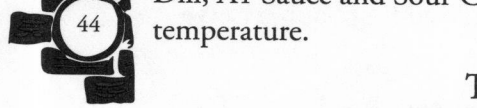

Heat the Burgundy Mushroom Gravy in a sauce pot. Add the Dill, A1 Sauce and Sour Cream to the sauce pot and bring to temperature.

Tuscan Sauce

This is one of Jeff's original sauces. The addition of the carrots and the cream takes the "edge" off the acidity of the tomatoes.

2 TBSP Vegetable Base
2 Cups Warm Water
1 tsp Sugar

1 ½ TBSP Canola Oil
1 TBSP Tomato Paste

1 ¼ Cup Yellow Onions, diced
1 ¼ Cups Carrots, half moon
2 Tomatoes, medium dice
½ tsp Kosher Salt
¾ tsp Black Pepper, coarse grind
⅛ tsp Cayenne Pepper
⅛ tsp Tabasco

2 TBSP Garlic, minced
2 TBSP Oregano
2 TBSP Thyme
1 ½ TBSP Masa Harina flour

2 Cups White Wine dry

¼ Cup + 1 TBSP Whipping Cream

Dissolve the Vegetable Base and Sugar in the Warm Water. Set aside for use later.

In a sauce pot, heat the Canola Oil over medium high heat. Add the Tomato Paste flattening it into a thin layer. Cook for about 2 minutes.

Add the Vegetables, Spices and Tabasco and sauté until the Onions are golden.

Add the Garlic, Spices and Masa and continue to sauté for another three minutes.

Add the wine, scraping the bottom of the pan to deglaze, continue cooking until reduced by half.

Add the Veggie stock, bring to a boil. Remove. When cool, puree in a blender or in a food processor. Place the puree back in the saucepan and add the Whipping Cream, bring back to temperature.

Yield is 4 Cups.

Kung Pao Sauce

This sauce we created for our Thai Chili Pork Sandwich, a late comer to our sandwich roster and a most welcome one!

1 TBSP Canola Oil
3 TBSP Garlic, minced
2 TBSP Ginger, minced

2 TBSP Sambal Oelek

1 Cup Dark Soy Sauce

4 TBSP Granulated Sugar
½ Cup Rice Vinegar

1 TBSP Cornstarch
1 tsp Water

Heat the Oil over high heat in a sauce pan and add the Garlic and Ginger. Sauté for one minute to soften.

Add the Sambal Oelek and sauté until well blended.

Add the Soy Sauce to deglaze the sauce pan, then add the Sugar and Rice Vinegar. Bring to a boil.

In a separate bowl, mix the Cornstarch and Water to make a slurry.

Add the slurry slowly to the sauce pan to thicken the sauce.

Check for flavor and season with Kosher Salt and Pepper if necessary .   Yield is 2 ½ Cups.

❧Shared Memories!

Thank you for always having the quality foods over all these years. Coming from Council and avoiding "junk food" while attending teacher trainings, I loved the food and easy location. Thank you for your excellent service and great servers. I loved the local artists featured, too. All great things must end...one door closes and another opens. You will be missed. Nina from Council.

And from one of the artists

In 2012, Steve Taylor wrote
"Two years ago you graciously hosted my artwork at Brick Oven and I've been oil painting every since. The whole experience (colors, great food then and now) inspired me, and I recently completed and entered a painting based on your patio called "Springtime in Boise" into this year's Western Idaho Fair. It won first place and can be viewed at www.chromebrush.com."

We had the great good fortune to host so many talented artists over the years. Along with the Capitol City Public Market, the City Department of Arts and History, Boise Blue and the Boise Weekly, we hosted the weekly "Emerging Artist's Exhibit". Its mission was "to promote the arts by assisting and encouraging local artists with little or no show experience by providing weekly exhibit opportunities not otherwise available."

To all the artists, Thank you for enriching our lives!

Our Salads

Hand Carved Salads and Vegetarian Salads were the first salad platters that we offered. We continued to use the name Vegetarian Salad, however after the umpteenth "Do you have a Chef's Salad?", our Hand Carved was renamed!

Our choice of greens varied with the season and availability. The addition of marinated English Cucumbers was the happy result of a period of time when finding Tomatoes was difficult and the quality dreadful. We have always been proponents of "When life sends you lemons, make Lemonade." Our Muffuletta topping and our scratch made Salad Dressings, we believe, lent our salads a wonderful distinction from others we taste!

Bistro Salads

Bistro Chef's Salad - Organic Greens, Sliced Tomato, Sliced marinated English Cucumber, sliced hardboiled Egg, Hand Carved Meat of your choice, shredded Cheese, Muffuletta

Bistro Vegetarian Salad - Organic Greens, Sliced Tomato, Sliced marinated English Cucumber, sliced hardboiled Egg, shredded Cheese, Muffuletta

Bistro Caesar Salad - Dressed shirred Romaine, freshly baked Croutons, Parmesan Cheese

Bistro Caesar & Meat Salad - Dressed shirred Romaine, Hand Carved Meat of your choice, freshly baked Croutons, Parmesan Cheese

Club Salad Platter - Organic Greens, Sliced Tomato, Sliced marinated English Cucumber, sliced Mushrooms, Hand Carved Turkey, shredded Cheese, Ranch Dressing & Bacon Bits

Our Dressing choices were Citrus Vinaigrette, Pepper Parmesan, Ranch and our Traditional Caesar! Their recipes follow:

Fresh Citrus Vinaigrette

This dressing was tart and perfect on our greens topped with Muffuletta. It is important to use fresh lemons and limes and squeeze them as you make this. The flavor difference between using fresh and bottled is great, and for the little time it takes to cut and squeeze them well worth it!

A good friend shared with us once that to get the most juice she micro waved the whole fruit prior to cutting for 10 seconds. Indeed this does soften them and produce more juice. The choice is yours!

½ Cup Apple Cider Vinegar
1 TBSP Lime Juice, fresh squeezed
3 TBSP Lemon Juice, fresh squeezed

2 tsp Kosher Salt
⅛ tsp White Pepper
⅛ tsp Black Pepper, coarse grind
Dash Cayenne Pepper

1 TBSP Parsley, chopped
4 tsp Dijon Mustard
4 tsp Honey, local if possible

1 Cup Olive Oil
1 Cup Canola Oil

Beat all ingredients except the oils with a whisk or in a mixer for about two minutes, scraping the sides to make sure the dry ingredients are dissolved.

Add the Oils slowly until fully blended.

Yield is 2 ½ Cups

Pepper Parmesan Dressing

Always our "House Dressing", this recipe was a winner from the beginning. We also used this dressing in our Parmesan Chicken and Parmesan Turkey Sandwiches. The flavors continue to delight and we continue to make this at home, where we use it for green salads as well as new pasta, quinoa and rice salads!

1 ½ tsp Anchovy Paste
4 tsp A-1 Sauce

¼ tsp Dijon Mustard
2 TBSP Lemon Juice, fresh squeezed
½ tsp Maggi Seasoning
6 TBSP Worcestershire Sauce

½ tsp Onion Powder
½ tsp Black Pepper, coarse grind
1 ¾ tsp White Sugar
4 ½ TBSP Parmesan Cheese

2 TBSP Parsley, finely chopped

2 Cups Mayonnaise

Beat the Anchovy Paste and the A-1 sauce with a whisk or in a mixer until the Anchovy Paste is fully dissolved and there are no lumps.

Add the remaining ingredients and whisk or mix until completely blended.   Yield is 2 ½ Cups

Ranch Dressing

There are ranch dressings and then there is ours! If you look at other recipes you'll see that once again the layers of flavor are many. It really is in the details!

½ Cup Sour Cream
¼ Cup Buttermilk

1 ½ TBSP Parmesan Cheese
4 tsp White Sugar
¾ tsp Dry Mustard
½ tsp Black Pepper, coarse grind
¼ tsp Kosher Salt

¾ tsp Apple Cider Vinegar
Dash Tabasco
4 tsp Worcestershire Sauce

¼ tsp Garlic, chopped
1 ½ TBSP Red Onion, diced
¾ tsp Lemon Juice, fresh squeezed

1 ½ Cups Mayonnaise

Beat the Sour Cream and the Buttermilk with a whisk or in a mixer until it is smooth and there are no lumps.

Add the remaining ingredients and whisk or mix until completely blended.

Yield is 2 ½ Cups

♣Shared Memories

Our boys, Jorden and Alex, grew up
eating at the Brick Oven Beanery/
Bistro. Both of them started
out riding around in the rolling
highchairs, then graduated to parents
telling them 'No, you can't climb on
the railing' while waiting in line.

By the time they were in elementary
school they knew their orders: a kids
meal with cheddar-veg soup, bread
and a cookie - maybe a pickle too -
and either lemonade or Orangina.
Over the years they moved on to full
size meals (but still cheddar veg soup).
Eventually we brought Jorden's
college friends to sit outside on an Alive After Five night.

We can't really decide which were our favorite times - summer
with lots of lemonade or a malt, or watching the snow fall on a
winter evening after the Mayor lit the Christmas tree.
All creating a lifetime of fond memories.

Sally Oberlindacher

Caesar Dressing

What follows is a very traditional recipe for a salad that both Jeff and I enjoyed growing up, when the waiter would come to the table and prepare the salad – something rare to see these days! We also used this dressing in our Chicken or Turkey Caesar Salad Sandwich. The dressing is best when made with extra virgin Olive Oil.

1 large Egg
5 ½ TBSP Lemon Juice, fresh squeezed
1 ½ tsp Worcestershire Sauce
½ tsp Anchovy Paste
1 ¾ tsp Garlic, chopped
¾ tsp table Salt
½ tsp White Pepper

1 Cup + 1 TBSP Olive Oil

Beat all the ingredients except for the Olive Oil with a whisk or in a mixer until it is smooth.

Slowly add the Olive Oil and whisk or mix until completely blended.

Yield is 1 ½ Cups

Applewood Smoked Potato Egg and Olive Salad

Originally this salad was made with plain Hardboiled Eggs. It was delicious and is delicious made this way. Unable to resist a new idea, we experimented smoking the Eggs added them to this salad and liked the taste even better. We leave it to you to choose your method!

Dressing:
2 TBSP Parsley, chopped
½ Cup Black Olives, sliced
½ Cup Red Onions, chopped

½ Cup Mayonnaise
½ tsp Horseradish
1 TBSP Salad Mustard
2 TBSP Dijon Mustard
½ tsp Tabasco

1 ½ tsp Celery Salt
¼ tsp Dill
½ tsp Paprika
½ tsp Black Pepper
⅛ tsp White Pepper
½ tsp Kosher Salt
1 TBSP Granulated Sugar

55

Salad:
2 Lbs Red Potatoes, cooked, ¼ " dice
½ Cup Celery chopped
4 Hardboiled Smoked Eggs, sliced

Make the Dressing by combining all the ingredients in a large bowl and mixing them thoroughly.

Place the cooked diced Red Potatoes, Celery and sliced Eggs into the bowl of Dressing and fold in carefully, so as not to smash the Potatoes or the Eggs!   Yield is 1 Quart.

Calico Bean Salad

Couldn't be easier to make! And for such ease you are rewarded with great flavor. For a variation, we have added Rotini pasta, or Brown Rice, each slightly different, both delicious.

Dressing:
1 ¼ tsp Garlic
Pinch Cayenne Pepper
¾ tsp Cumin
1 tsp Dry Mustard
1 tsp Black Pepper
1 tsp Kosher Salt
1 TBSP Granulated Sugar
2 TBSP Brown Sugar

2 ½ TBSP Cider Vinegar
dash Tabasco

⅓ Cup Olive Oil

Salad:
1 15 oz can Green Beans
1 15 oz can Pinto Beans
1 15 oz can Red Beans

⅔ Cup Parsley, chopped
1 tsp Jalapeno, minced

⅔ Cup Celery, sliced
⅔ Cup Red Onions, chopped

Dressing:
Place all the ingredients from the Garlic to the Tabasco in a large
bowl and whisk well.

Slowly drizzle the Olive Oil into the mixture in the bowl until it is
full incorporated. Set aside.

Salad:
Drain the liquid from all the Beans. Rinse them in cool water,
then drain and place them in a large bowl.
Add the Parsley, Jalapeno, Celery and Red Onions and fold
carefully so as not to break the beans.

Add the dressing and fold in completely. Cool, serve when chilled.
                                        Yield is 1 ½ Quarts.

Creamy Coleslaw

This coleslaw is great as a cold side dish and adds the perfect crunch and creaminess in our Slawich, Picadillo and Thai Chile Pork Sandwiches.

Dressing:
½ Cup Sour Cream
1 Cup Mayonnaise

1 TBSP Cider Vinegar
1 TBSP Lemon Juice
¼ tsp Tabasco
2 tsp Worcestershire Sauce
½ tsp Dijon Mustard

½ tsp Caraway Seed
Dash Cayenne Pepper
¼ tsp Celery Seed
½ tsp Black Pepper, coarse grind
½ tsp White Pepper
1 tsp Kosher Salt
¾ tsp Granulated Sugar

Place the Sour Cream and the Mayonnaise in a large bowl and whisk well.

Add all the other ingredients to the bowl and whisk until smooth.

Yield is 1 ¾ Cups.

Salad: To make the Creamy Coleslaw, use ½ to ¾ cup of Dressing for 1 Lb. of Slaw mix. We used a mix of White Cabbage, Red Cabbage with a touch of Carrots in ours.

Blushing Applesauce

A favorite with many of our younger guests, it won over many an adult as well. We remember parents dipping into their children's bowl, for "Just a taste!" This is great with a sandwich but equally as good with our Sunday Country Pork Roast Dinner.

    3 Lbs frozen Apples, thawed
    2 Cups Water

    7 ¼ Oz Raspberries, frozen
    ½ tsp Cinnamon

    1 ½ tsp Lemon juice, fresh squeezed
    ½ Cup White Sugar

Once the apples are thawed place them in a saucepan with the water. Cook them over medium heat until the apples are soft and tender, but not mushy.

Set the apples aside for at least 20 minutes to cool

Add the remaining ingredients and with a potato masher or a heavy duty whisk, mix until there are still a few lumps of apples but it is mostly smooth. Cool and serve!   Yield is 1 ½ Quarts.

Rum Pot Beans

Our re-definition of Baked Beans is here for you. These are great paired with our Applewood Smoked Potato Salad or our Creamy Coleslaw and one of our Sandwiches.

Day 1   Place the beans and water in a stock pot or container, cover and leave them to soak overnight.

> 1 Cup Red Beans, dried
> 1 Cup Pinto Beans, dried
> 2 tsp Kosher Salt
> 3 Qts Water

Day 2

> 2 tsp Beef Base
> ¼ Cup Water
>
> 2 Tbsp Molasses
> Dash Tabasco Sauce
> 2 ½ TBSP Worcestershire Sauce
> 2 ½ TBSP Dark Beer
> 2 tsp Dark Rum
> ¼ Cup V-8 Juice
> ½ Cup Ketchup
> 1 ½ TBSP Soy Sauce
>
> ¾ tsp Dry Mustard
> ¼ tsp Celery Salt

1 ½ TBSP Brown Sugar

½ tsp Garlic, minced
½ Cup Yellow Onions, diced
2 TBSP Bacon, cooked and diced

Wash and drain the soaked Beans and place them in a large stock pot. Cover them plenty of water. Bring to a boil and then simmer, uncovered until the Beans are tender, 3 to 4 hours.

Pre-heat the oven to 300 degrees.

Place the Beef Base and Water in a large bowl and dissolve the Base fully.

Place all the remaining ingredients in the bowl and mix the Bean Sauce completely.

When the Beans are tender, drain them and place them in a baking dish.

Add the Bean Sauce and gently mix until evenly distributed.

Cover tightly with aluminum foil and a lid.
Place in a preheated oven and bake until the Beans are tender and the Bean Sauce has been fully absorbed. Check and taste each hour. Baking will take 3 – 4 hours.

Yield is 2 ½ Quarts.

Worries go down better with soup.

Jewish Proverb

Many of our staff and guests were intrigued by the tastes we created in our soups. For some these tastes opened up a whole new world of food and possibility. And, we fulfilled one of our hopes, to raise the awareness of the richness of life!

Clearly it would be a wonderful universe if every soup or stew we made started with our own scratch made stock, wonderful and unrealistic! In the restaurant we always made our Lobster Stock for our Etouffee, as we could never find a Lobster Base we liked. When it came to Chicken, Beef and Vegetable Bases, we did find good ones, MSG free, produced by RL Schreiber & Co. Sadly, they are not a retail company, and thus their bases are not sold in local markets. One of our first tasks was to find a good retail base – we did! Superior Quality Foods makes a line of "Better Than Bouillon" bases, readily available in our local markets. We used these bases for all the recipes in this book. If you decide to go with another product, please be sure to taste what you choose to use. And, as always, read the ingredient list. Bases vary greatly in flavor and quality!

Vegetables for soups and stews are a topic of great interest to us. Over the twenty eight years, we watched as more and more restaurants were seduced away from cooking their own to buying production soups. Nearly every year, we would travel out of state to a restaurant conference, where we would taste the newest arrivals. We always came away disappointed. Large production soups fall victim to the economy of scale issues. All of the vegetables are sauteed at the same time and for the same length of time, vegetable sizes are uniform and then often they are frozen. Certainly methods of freezing have improved, but in our opinion, flavor was lost in the process.

We always have held to the old adage, you get out what you put in. You will see in the recipes that follow, ingredients are added at different times, carrots are half moon cut, cauliflower is in small florets, celery is sliced and only the onions chopped!

Next time you are served a soup, we invite you to consider this!

*"There is nothing better on a cold wintry day
than a properly made pot pie."*

Craig Claiborne

Pot Pies

Pillsbury Puff Pastries were our choice for making our Pot Pie crusts. They are very light and crisp and a great textural difference to the stews that we placed within them. We chose our stews for our Pot Pies from the many recipes we have included. Our favorites were the Shepard's and Hunter's, the inspiration for a blog in 2009, which we include with the recipes!

Cheddar Vegetable Chowder

Our notes and a lovely story in its honor follow the recipe!

Roux:
4 oz Butter
½ Cup All Purpose Flour

1 Cup Carrots, half rounds
1 Cup Celery, sliced
1 Cup Red Onions, chopped
1 Cup Broccoli, florets
1 Cup Cauliflower florets
1 Cup Zucchini, half rounds

2 TBSP Veggie Base
1 ½ Qts Water

10 oz Sharp Cheddar Cheese, grated
¾ Cup Milk
¾ Cup Heavy Cream

⅛ tsp Tabasco
½ tsp Worcestershire Sauce
½ tsp Granulated Sugar
¼ tsp White Pepper

Roux:
Melt the butter in a small sauce pan, add the flour and mix
well. Over low to medium heat, cook the roux for ten minutes,

adjusting the temperature of the burner, so that the roux cooks but does not brown. Set aside to cool for use later.

Steam the Vegetables separately or together at your preference. In order to steam them together, layer them at different times in your steamer, with the Carrots, Celery and Cauliflower on the bottom, then after a few minutes of steaming them alone, add the Broccoli for another few minutes, ending with the Zucchini and the Red Onions. When crisp tender set them aside for use later.

Place the Veggie Base and the Water in a sauce pot. Whisk thoroughly and over high heat, bring to a boil.

Add the Roux by the spoonful, whisking in completely before the next addition.

When all the Roux is added, and the stock is thick and smooth, reduce the heat to a simmer. Simmer for 15 minutes.

Add the Cheddar Cheese to the thickened Stock. Whisk in fully. Simmer for 5 minutes.

Add the Milk, Cream and Spices and simmer for an additional 5 minutes.

Add the cooked vegetables and mix in carefully.

Serve with a scoop of Hand Mashed Potatoes (Pg 157) in the center of the bowl.   Yield is 2 Quarts.

Our notes:

Known to most of you as Cheddar Veggie, this soup was originally introduced to our seasonal Winter menu in December of 1989. After the 10th request for Cheddar Veggie during the first day of the Spring Menu, Cheddar Veg was back on the menu and it became one of the most loved items, all seasons of the year!

66

The original version we made with grated Sharp Wisconsin Cheddar Cheese as written here. As the years went on, we made this soup with a Sharp Cheddar Spread, a product which we have not found on the shelves of our retail stores.

Shared Memories!

After I moved to Boise I decided to do the Boise half Ironman. I had just finished the race and I was wandering through the Grove very tired and slightly confused when a volunteer asked me if I would like some soup. I don't remember responding to her question before she handed me the cheddar vegetable chowder with a scoop of mashed potatoes (one of my favorite foods) on top. My only thought was "Boise is the best town ever-- they even put mashed potatoes in their soup!" Every race I do I think of that soup and how it was the perfect post-race meal-- so delicious and cheesy!   Leslie Smith

Chicken Stock

Chicken Backs are inexpensive and readily available at meat markets in town. They make a great Chicken Stock. Often at home, we buy a whole chicken and cut it up, saving the Backs in the freezer for making this stock. Chicken purchased this way is far more economical and it gives you the makings for this stock.

3 ½ Lbs Chicken Backs

3 Gal Water
2 Pcs Bay Leaves
4 Pcs Black Peppercorns

1 ½ Cups Yellow Onions, coarsely chopped
1 ½ Cups Carrots, coarsely chopped
1 ½ Cups Celery, coarsely chopped
1 Cup Parsley Stems

Place the Chicken Backs and all the ingredients in a large stock pot. Bring to a boil, then reduce to a simmer. Simmer for 3 hours. Skim the surface every 20 minutes to remove any foam that collects.

After 3 hours, taste the stock. If needed, simmer for a half an hour longer. Remove from the heat and strain carefully.

Place in the refrigerator and the next day, skim the fat off the surface.

Yield is 2 Gallons.

Chicken or Turkey Rice Soup

3 TBSP Olive Oil

1 tsp Garlic
⅔ Cup Carrots, half rounds
⅔ Cup Celery, sliced
⅔ Cup Yellow Onions, chopped

1 ½ TBSP Chicken Base
1 ¾ Qts Water

½ tsp Basil
Pinch Cayenne Pepper
⅛ tsp Black Pepper
¾ tsp Thyme
¼ tsp Tabasco

½ Lb Chicken / Turkey, cooked and diced in ½ inch cubes

Heat the Olive Oil over medium heat. Add the Garlic, Carrots, Celery and Yellow onions and sauté until they are tender.

Dissolve the Chicken Base in the Water and add to the sauce pot. Add the Spices to the sauce pot, bring to a boil, then reduce the heat to a simmer.
Add the cooked Chicken or Turkey and simmer for 15 minutes.

Serve with a scoop of Veggie Rice (Pg 160) placed in the centre of the bowl.   Yield is 2 Quarts.

Mrs. Beeton's Kitchen Maxims

If you took a look around our kitchen you might have seen this timeless advice from a woman considered Victorian England's answer to Martha Stewart, Isabella Beeton.

There is no work like early work.

A good manager looks ahead.

Clear as you go. Muddle makes more muddle.

Not to wash plates and dishes soon after using makes more work.

Dirty saucepans filled with hot water begin to clean themselves.

Roast meat should start in a hot oven.

Water boils when it gallops, oil when it is still.

Put spare crusts in the oven to grate for bread crumbs,

Salt brings out flavors.

One egg, beaten well, is worth two not beaten.

A stew boiled is a stew spoiled.

As our staff would share, these were only the start of our frequently repeated morsels of wisdom, the concepts of our universe!

Chicken or Turkey Dill Soup

A light soup full of flavor, we topped this with our Veggie Rice. This is a very versatile recipe. We often substituted Tarragon for the Dill, left out the Marjoram, and thus had a Chicken or Turkey Tarragon Soup.

1 ½ TBSP Canola Oil
2 Cups Red Onions, diced
2 Cups Yellow Onions, diced
2 Cups Carrots, diced
2 Cups Celery, diced

¼ Cup Dry Vermouth

1 ½ TBSP Chicken Base
2 ½ Qts Water

⅓ Cup Green Onions, chopped
⅓ Cup Parsley, chopped
1 TBSP Dill Weed
1 ½ tsp Marjoram
¼ tsp Black Pepper, coarse grind
¼ tsp White Pepper
Pinch Cayenne
1 ½ tsp Granulated Sugar
¼ tsp Tabasco

⅔ Lb Chicken/Turkey, cooked and diced in ½ inch cubes

Heat the Canola Oil in a sauce pot over medium heat. Add the Red Onions, Yellow Onions, Carrots, Celery and sauté until they are tender but not browned.

Deglaze the sauce pot with the Vermouth, making sure to scrape the bottom of the sauce pot clean.

Mix the Chicken Base completely into the Water and add to the Veggies in the sauce pot.

Add the Green Onions, Parsley and the Spices to the sauce pot. Bring to a boil, then reduce the heat to a simmer. Simmer until the Veggies are tender.

Add the cooked Chicken or Turkey and simmer for 15 minutes.

Serve with a scoop of Veggie Rice (pg 160) placed in the centre of the bowl.

Yield is 3 Quarts.

Every week, with the paychecks came the "Bean Bulletin", each week, new material. Often we included comments from folks in our industry - like this lovely comment by Sam Choy, a wonderful Hawaiian chef/owner whom we had the great good fortune of eating with and meeting - "I believe you can learn something every day, no matter where you are or what you're doing. " <u>Cooking from the Heart</u>

Chicken or Turkey Pepperpot

Full flavored and a bit spicy, this soup is delicious with a scoop of our Veggie Rice!

1 TBSP Chicken Base
1 Qt Water

½ Cup Dry Vermouth
½ tsp Granulated Sugar
⅛ tsp Tabasco

¾ TBSP Garlic, chopped
¼ tsp Black Peppercorns, whole
⅛ tsp Green Peppercorns
1 Bay Leaf

¼ tsp Black Pepper
¼ tsp Cayenne
⅛ tsp White Pepper
¼ tsp Marjoram
¼ tsp Thyme

¼ Cup Carrots, half moon
½ Cup Celery, chopped
⅓ Cup Red Onion, chopped
⅓ Cup Yellow Onion, chopped

2 TBSP Parsley, chopped
½ Cup Green Peppers, chopped
¼ Cup Roasted Red Peppers, drained, rinsed & chopped
2 TBSP Scallions, chopped

½ Lb Chicken or Turkey, cooked and chopped in ¼" cubes

Place the Chicken Base, Water, Vermouth, Sugar, Tabasco, Garlic and all the spices in a sauce pot and bring to a boil.

Add all of the Vegetables and the Chicken and bring the soup back to a boil. Reduce the heat and simmer for 10 minutes or until all the vegetables are crisp tender.

♣Wild Rice

One of the challenges and delights was finding the right products! We purchased our Wild Rice blend from a wonderful company in Wisconsin, Chieftain Wild Rice. They are a remarkable company for the quality of the products they create and the customer service that they provide. They have so many unique products and recipes. We used their Chef's Top Blend, which was a combination of Dry Roasted Wild Rice and Parboiled Brown Rice. The way this blend worked, most importantly in our Wild Rice Meatloaf, made us loyal customers. This soup that follows was inspired by them and tweaked by us! We encourage you to visit their website www.chieftainwildrice.com and to order and try their products.

Chippewa Lakes Chicken or Turkey Wild Rice

Roux:
4 TBSP Butter
⅓ Cup All Purpose Flour

1 ½ Cups cooked Chieftian Chef's Top Blend Wild Rice
(½ Cup Dry)

1 TBSP Canola Oil
⅓ Cup Carrots, half moon cut
⅓ Cup Celery, chopped
2 TBSP Green Pepper, chopped
⅓ Cup Yellow Onion, chopped

¾ Cup Mushrooms, sliced
1 ¼ tsp Jalapeno pepper, minced

2 TBSP Roasted Red Peppers, chopped
¾ Cup Creamed Corn
¼ Cup Corn kernels
2 TBSP Dry Sherry

1 TBSP Chicken Base
1 ½ Qts Water

⅛ tsp Cayenne Pepper
¼ tsp Black Pepper
¼ tsp Nutmeg
½ Lb. Chicken or Turkey, cooked and chopped

3 TBSP Whipping Cream

Roux:

Melt the butter in a small sauce pan, add the flour and mix
well. Over low to medium heat, cook the roux for ten minutes,
adjusting the temperature of the burner, so that the roux cooks but
does not brown. Set aside to cool for use later.

Place the Oil in a sauce pot over medium heat. Add the Carrot,
Celery, Green Pepper and Yellow Onion and sauté until the Onion
is tender.

Add the Mushrooms and Jalapeno to the other veggies in the sauce
pot and sauté until the Mushrooms are golden. Reduce the heat to
low.

75

Add the Red Pepper, Creamed Corn, Corn Kernels and Sherry and
cook for 4 minutes.
Remove from the heat, reserve to add later.

Place the Chicken Base and the Water in a sauce pot over high
heat and whisk fully.

When boiling add the Roux, whisk until smooth. Reduce the heat
and simmer until thickened.

Add the reserved Veggie Mix to the sauce pot.

Add the Spices, the Chicken or Turkey, Wild Rice and Whipping
Cream to the sauce pot. Bring to temperature, taste for seasoning
and adjust as necessary.   Yield is 2 Quarts.

Thai Chicken or Turkey Soup

We were so delighted when the first Thai restaurants came to Boise. Both Jeff and I have enjoyed Thai food in many different locations over our lives. When we discovered and experimented with this recipe, we loved it for its lightness and rich flavor. It is also such an easy recipe to make that our cooks loved it for those days when the list seemed to just grow and we needed yet another soup.

2 Qts Water
¼ Cup Chicken Base

1 Qt Chicken, cooked and diced (or Turkey)
1 Qt Carrots, peeled and shredded

1 Can (13.5 oz) Coconut Milk
½ Cup Lime Juice
2 tsp Sesame Oil

1 ½ tsp Cayenne Pepper
2 tsp Coriander, ground
2 tsp Garlic Powder
2 tsp Ginger, ground

Place the Water and Chicken Base in a medium sized sauce pot and whisk until the Chicken Base is completely dissolved.

Add Chicken or Turkey and Carrots and bring to a boil

Once boiling, reduce to a simmer and add the Coconut Milk, Lime Juice and Sesame Oil.

Add the spices and simmer for about 30 minutes.

Serve with Veggie Rice (Pg 160).   Yield is 1 ¼ Gallons.

Coq au Vin Bistro style

You never know where a culinary inspiration is going to come from…or just how it might influence what you do in the kitchen.

Take our soup for this week, Coq au Vin. Those of you familiar with this particular French dish know that more than your taste buds get into the mix when you bring a spoonful up to your mouth. Your olfactory sense is bathed in the Burgundy wine that is a key ingredient in the soup base, and that flavor and its accompanying aroma coat your throat and your sinuses as your taste buds begin to pick up on the chicken, bacon, mushrooms and onions in the broth. As Dylan would say, "something's going on here, but you don't know what it is, do you, Mr. Jones."

So, just what is that something? The answer, oddly enough, comes not only from France, but also from Japan. Permit us to explain.

As far back as the ancient Greek philosophers, the conventional gastronomical and anatomical wisdom was that humans could detect four distinct tastes: sweet, sour, salty, and bitter. Even as

medical science evolved, the belief continued that our receptors were limited to these four tastes.

It took legendary French chef Auguste Escoffier, and his creation of veal stock in the late 1800's, to prove that we humans could taste an indefinable deliciousness that scientists at the time simply concluded was all in our heads. Halfway around the world, however, a Japanese chemist named Kikunae Ikeda proved that this taste was, in fact, related to a previously undiscovered receptor. This "fifth taste" was given the name umami – Japanese for (appropriately enough), "yummy". The dish that inspired Ikeda's research was the classic Japanese soup made from seaweed, dashi.

Umami is, in fact, L-glutamate. Quoting from a recent National Public Radio story, "L-glutamate is found in most living things, but when they die, when organic matter breaks down, the glutamate molecule breaks apart. This can happen on a stove when you cook meat, over time when you age a Parmesan cheese, by fermentation as in soy sauce or under the sun as a tomato ripens. When glutamate becomes L-glutamate, that's when things get 'delicious.' L-glutamate, said Ikeda, is a fifth taste. When Escoffier created veal stock, he was concentrating umami. When Japanese made their dashi, they were doing the same thing."

So now you know an interesting piece of culinary and scientific trivia. But more than that, we've just given you some insight into how we do what we do in the Brick Oven Bistro kitchen when we make a soup like our Coq au Vin. Next time you take a bite, you might want to observe a moment of silent praise for Auguste

Escoffier and Kikunae Ikeda. Then impress your fellow diners with the statement, "this soup tastes absolutely umami!"

> 1 TBSP Canola Oil
> ¾ Cup Yellow Onions, chopped
> 1 ½ Cups Mushrooms, sliced
> 2 tsp Garlic, chopped
>
> 1 ½ tsp Brandy
>
> 1 TBSP Beef Base
> 5 Cups Water, hot
>
> 1 ½ Cups Red Wine, dry
> 1 Bay Leaf
> ¼ tsp Black Pepper
> Dash Cayenne Pepper
> Dash White Pepper
> ¼ tsp Thyme
> 2 TBSP Parsley, chopped
>
> ½ Lb Chicken, cooked and diced
> ¼ Lb Bacon, cooked and chopped

Heat the Canola Oil in a sauce pot over low heat. Add the Onions, Mushrooms and Garlic and sauté until the Onions are just golden.

Do not burn the Garlic! - Whenever we say this, we hear the voice of Pierre Franey in the background! He often said this in his early videos that we enjoyed watching!

Add the Brandy to the sauce pot and sauté until most of the liquor is burned off.

Dissolve the Beef Base in the hot Water and add to the sauce pot.

Add the Red Wine and the Spices to the sauce pot. Bring it to a boil, then reduce the heat.

Add the Chicken and Bacon and simmer over low heat for 45 minutes.   Yield is 2 Quarts.

Italian Wedding Soup

Thank goodness for heritage! We enjoy reading Saveur Magazine as more than any other, it brings the world to Boise! This family special (Steph's) calls for Curly Endive, which is sometimes hard to find. This soup is tasty as well with Arugula or a mix of Arugula and Spinach.

> 1 ½ TBSP Chicken Base
> 6 Cups Water
>
> ½ Lb Curly Endive, chopped
> ½ Lb Meatballs (roll each meatball to size using ½ tsp)
>
> 1 Egg, Large
> 1 TBSP Parmesan Cheese, freshly grated
>
> ¼ tsp Black Pepper, coarse grind

Place the Chicken Base and the Water in a sauce pot over medium high heat. Whisk until the Base is fully dissolved.

Bring to a boil. Reduce the heat to a simmer.

Add the Curly Endive and Meatballs to the broth and simmer for 8 minutes.

Place the Egg and the Parmesan Cheese in a small bowl and whisk well.

Stir the broth in a circular motion. Gradually drizzle the egg mixture into the moving broth, stirring gently to form thin strands of egg, about 1 minute.

Taste for seasoning and adjust as desired. Top with grated Parmesan Cheese. Yield is 1 Quart.

♣Just Nike it!

In the course of a day, anything could happen and often did. This was often the final conclusion we reached and comment we shared with staff as to how we were going to proceed - a man down, the ice machine broken, repair person on the way and someone running to get ice, and doors to open! Running a restaurant is not unlike sailing around the world. We thank the Oregon shoe folks for inspiring us!

Beef Vegetable Soup

Light and flavorful, this was dinner for us on many a night after a long day. Soup making is a wonderful, creative experience that we hope, like us, you all will enjoy often!

82

1 TBSP Olive Oil
¾ Cup Yellow Onions, diced
½ tsp Garlic

1 TBSP Beef Base
1 ½ Qts Water

¾ Cup Carrots, coin cut
¾ Cup Cauliflower, small florets
¾ Cup Celery, sliced
¾ Cup Green Beans, 1" pieces

¼ tsp Oregano
Pinch Cayenne Pepper
⅛ tsp Black Pepper, coarse grind
½ tsp Thyme
¼ tsp Maggi Seasoning
Dash Tabasco

½ Lb Beef, cooked and cut into half inch cubes

Heat the Olive Oil over medium heat in a sauce pot. Add the Onions and the Garlic and sauté until golden.

Mix the Beef Base with the Water and add to the sauce pot.

Add the Carrots, Celery, Cauliflower and Green Beans as well as the Spices to the sauce pot. Bring to a boil and then reduce the heat to a simmer. Simmer until the veggies are just tender.

Add the Beef and simmer for an additional 15 – 20 minutes.

Taste and adjust seasoning.

Serve with a scoop of Veggie Rice (Pg 160) in the centre.
Yield is 2 Quarts.

❧ *Shared Memories!*

Our family has such precious memories of your special restaurant! We moved to Boise in 1989 when our kids were still little and found your restaurant - at it's original location - to be such a fun place to hang out and get such yummy food! We were always greeted with such enthusiasm and felt very comfortable, especially with our little flock!
When you moved to the new location, your outdoor water fountain/pool was a welcome splash for our kids in the summertime and your lemon chicken + mashed potatoes with corn gravy + salad our family favorite! Thanks a million!
Dean and Angela Schurger, with Melissa, Tasha and Caleb

Portuguese Kale & Sausage Soup

This soup is best made a day ahead of serving, so that the flavors have some time to meld. The idea for this soup came after a visit from family. Our families love to cook and love to share recipes. We cherish our mealtime gatherings, when the food is fabulous and the conversations spirited!

1 TBSP Olive Oil

½ Lb Kielbasa Sausage, ½ inch slice
1 Cup Yellow Onion, diced

1 ½ tsp Garlic, minced

2 TBSP Chicken Base
2 Qts Water

2 TBSP Parsley, chopped
1 Bay Leaf
1 tsp Mint
¼ tsp Red Pepper Flakes
¼ tsp Thyme
¼ tsp Kosher Salt

2 Cups Kale, washed, trimmed and chopped

¾ Cup Red Potatoes, peeled and diced

1 Cup Red Beans, cooked

Heat the Olive Oil over medium heat. Add the sliced Sausage and Yellow onions and sauté for about 3 minutes.

Add the Garlic and sauté for 2 minutes .

Mix the Chicken Base completely into the Water and add to the Veggies in the sauce pot.

Add the Parsley, Spices and Kale to the sauce pot, bring to a boil, then reduce the heat to a simmer, and simmer for about 35 minutes, until the Kale is quite tender.

Add the Red Potatoes and Red Beans and simmer for an additional 15 minutes.

Cool overnight and reheat over medium heat. Taste and adjust seasonings.   Yield is 1 ¾ Quarts.

Chowder breathes reassurance.

It steams consolation.

Clementine Paddleford

Bistro Corn Chowder

As promised, here it is! We would make phone calls to let folks know that indeed, this was on the menu that day. It was always about taking the extra step forward.

Roux:
3 TBSP Butter
1 Cup Yellow Onions, diced
½ Cup + 2 TBSP All Purpose Flour

1 TBSP Chicken Base
1 Qt + 2 Cups Water

¾ tsp White Pepper
1 ¼ tsp Marjoram
Dash Nutmeg
1 Cup Red Potatoes, ½" dice
¼ Cup Carrots, half round

2 ¼ Cups Creamed Corn
½ Lb frozen Corn
¼ Cup Bacon, cooked and diced
¼ Cup + 2 TBSP Parsley, chopped
¼ Cup Milk
¼ Cup Heavy Cream
¾ tsp Kosher Salt
¼ tsp Black Pepper

Roux:

Melt the butter in a small saucepan, add the flour and mix well. Over low to medium heat, cook the roux for ten minutes, adjusting the temperature of the burner, so that the roux cooks but does not brown. Set aside for use later.

Place the Chicken Base, Water, Pepper Marjoram and Nutmeg in a stock pot and whisk together until completely mixed.

Place the Red Potatoes and the Carrots into the stock pot, bring to a boil and then reduce the heat to a simmer and simmer for 15 minutes, or until the Potatoes and the Carrots are crisp tender. Bring the stock pot back to a boil and add the Roux to the boiling stock a little at a time, whisking completely between additions. Stir constantly. When all the Roux is incorporated and the stock is thickened, reduce the heat to a simmer.

Add the remaining ingredients. Bring back to temperature, taste for seasoning and adjust as desired.

Yield is 2 Quarts.

❧ *Immediate Gratification!*

One of the most lovely conditions of owning a restaurant was that we received immediate feedback on our food and service. So many times in life, we do things and never really know the result. We did not have to wait for the end of the term to get our report card, we received our grades daily! And, we appreciated this!

Bistro Split Pea Soup

An American classic to which we added our own spicing twists. We made this in two and four gallon batches. When we reduce the recipe to two quarts as we have here, some of the spices seem to be in such small quantities that you might wonder if leaving them out would matter, it does!

1 Ham Hock

2 ½ Cups Green Split Peas
1 ¾ Qts Water

5 Oz Kielbasa Sausage, sliced half moon

⅓ Cup Yellow Onions, chopped
¾ Cup Carrots, chopped
¼ Cup Celery, chopped
2 TBSP Parsley, chopped

2 TBSP Chicken Base
2 TBSP Red Wine, dry
⅛ tsp Dry Mustard
⅛ tsp Thyme
⅛ tsp Kosher Salt
¼ tsp Black Pepper, coarse grind
¾ tsp Brown Sugar
1 Bay Leaf

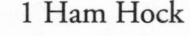

Soak the Ham Hock in enough milk to cover, for 30 minutes, then rinse and place in the sauce pot with the Split Peas, Water and Kielbasa Sausage.

Add all the ingredients to the sauce pot, bring them to a boil, then reduce the heat and simmer until the Split Peas are cooked, approximately one hour.

Before serving, remove the Ham Hock from the soup. Dice any Ham that you remove from the Ham Hock and add it to the sauce pot.

Remove the Bay Leaf prior to serving, or give a prize to the person who finds the Bay Leaf in their bowl!

♣Shared Memory dear to us!

Great Memories of the Brick Oven Bistro....and a little match making by owners Jeff and Stephanie and my daughter Karen!

Not only enjoying the Adventures of Comfort Food...but comforting and special memories of meeting my late husband Gary on the patio, a late September evening enjoying the soothing sounds of Jazz on the Grove. RoseMarie Frost

Creamy German Potato

This soup is ultimate comfort food raised to a new level. The spicing of it, toasting the whole Caraway Seeds and then grinding them and the addition of the Lemon Zest and Lemon Juice separate this from many a potato soup that we have tried.

I tsp Caraway Seed, whole

1 TBSP Canola Oil

1 tsp Garlic, minced
2 Cups Yellow Onions, diced
2 Cups Celery, diced

½ tsp Dried Mustard

1 TBSP Chicken Base
1 Qt Water

1 ½ Lbs Idaho Potatoes, peeled, 1" dice

¼ Cup Sour Cream
½ Cup Milk
½ Cup Whipping Cream

Pinch White Pepper
½ tsp Dill Weed
¼ Cup Parsley
Dash Tabasco

½ tsp Lemon Zest
2 tsp Lemon Juice

⅓ Lb Bacon, cooked and diced

Toast the Caraway seeds in a sauce pan over medium low heat, until they become fragrant but do not burn. Grind them by hand or in a spice grinder. Set aside for use later.

Heat the Canola Oil in a stock pot over medium high heat.

Add the Garlic, Onions and Celery and sauté until the Onions are golden.

Add the ground Caraway and the dried Mustard to the sautéed vegetables and cook for two minutes.

Mix the Chicken Base fully with the Water and add to the stock pot.

Add the Potatoes, raise the heat to high and bring to a boil. Reduce the heat to a simmer and cook until the Potatoes are soft.

Place the mixture in a blender and blend until mostly smooth. A few small lumps of Potatoes are fine!

Return the blended mixture to the stock pot, heat on medium low.

Add the Sour Cream, Milk and Heavy Cream and mix thoroughly.

Add the Spices, Lemon Zest, Lemon Juice and Bacon and bring up to temperature. Taste and adjust seasoning as desired.

Yield is 2 Quarts.

Autumn Squash Soup

Although the name implies a season, this soup is equally as good warm or chilled and thus can be served in any season! We are very fond of this served topped with homemade seasoned Croutons or crisp browned butter Sage leaves.

3 Lbs Butternut Squash, or your favorite yellow squash
2 TBSP Olive Oil

1 Qt Water
1 TBSP Chicken Base

½ tsp Nutmeg
Pinch Cayenne Pepper
½ tsp White Pepper
½ tsp Kosher Salt

½ Cup Heavy Cream

1 ½ Cups Ham, diced in ¼ inch cubes
1 ½ TBSP Butter

Pre-heat the oven to 400 degrees.

Cut the Squash in half and remove seeds. Brush Squash with Oil and place skin side down on a baking sheet. Roast for 35 – 45 minutes until slightly browned and soft. Cool and remove the skin from the Squash. Place the Squash in a large sauce pot.

Mix the Chicken Base with the Water until completely dissolved and add to the Squash in the sauce pot.

Add the Spices to the sauce pot. Heat over high heat until boiling, then reduce the heat and simmer for 15 minutes.

Blend the soup until smooth using a hand blender or placing the soups in batches in a blender. Return the soup to the sauce pot.

Add the Heavy Cream and whisk until smooth. Add the Ham and simmer for 15 minutes.

Add the Butter and mix in completely. Serve. Yield is 2 Quarts.

To make the Crisp Browned Butter Sage leaves, simply place butter in a sauce pan, melt over medium high heat. Add fresh Sage Leaves and cook them and the butter until the butter is browned and the Sage leaves are crisp.

❧Delighting your eyes and other tricks of the trade!

One of the things we struggled with was the color of our Cream of Broccoli Soup. The flavor was great, but too often the color was not! Our great thanks go to Alice Waters and Chez Panisse for their brilliant idea to cook the Broccoli to mush, to extract the full flavor and then to add Spinach to improve the color. When we tried this technique, we were delighted with the results.

Cream of Broccoli Soup

Roux:
6 TBSP Butter
½ Cup Flour

Soup:
2 TBSP Butter
½ Cup Yellow Onions, chopped
½ tsp Garlic, minced

3 TBSP Vegetable Base
4 ¼ Cups Water

⅛ tsp Cayenne Pepper
¾ Tsp White Pepper
¾ tsp Kosher Salt

¾ Lb Broccoli florets
¼ Cup Spinach, thawed and drained, frozen or fresh
spinach

1 ½ Cups Milk, whole
1 ½ Cups Heavy Cream

1 TBSP Lemon Juice

Roux:
Melt the butter in a small sauce pan, add the flour and mix well. Over low to medium heat, cook the roux for ten minutes, adjusting the temperature of the burner, so that the roux cooks but does not brown. Set aside for use later.

In a sauce pot, melt the Butter. Add the Onions and Garlic and sauté until just softened and not starting to color.

Dissolve the Vegetable Base fully in the water and then add to the sauteed vegetables in the sauce pot.

Add the Peppers and the Kosher Salt.

Add the Broccoli florets to the sauce pot, bring to a boil, reduce to a simmer and cook until they are mush.

Reduce the heat, add the Spinach and cook for 5 minutes.

Blend the soup until smooth using a hand blender or placing the soups in batches in a blender. Return the soup to the sauce pot.

Add the Milk and Heavy Cream and whisk until smooth.

Add the Lemon Juice, taste and adjust seasoning.

Serve topped with grated Parmesan Cheese.

                              Yield is 2 Quarts.

Lentil & 2 Pepper Soup

This vegetarian soup is tasty and when paired with rice becomes a good source of protein. We like its simplicity and its combination of flavors. Using a good Vegetable stock or base is key!

¼ Cup Olive Oil

2 TBSP Garlic, minced
¾ Cup Yellow Onions, diced
½ Cup Carrots, coin cut

1 TBSP Vegetable Base
6 Cups Water

¾ Cup Lentils

1 Cup Red Peppers, diced
1 Cup Green Peppers, diced

½ Cup Dry Sherry
Pinch Cayenne Pepper
¼ tsp White Pepper
¼ tsp Black Pepper, coarse grind
½ tsp Salt

Heat the Olive Oil over medium high heat in a sauce pot.

Add the Garlic, Onions and Carrots and sauté until tender.

Mix the Vegetable Base and the Water completely and add to the sauce pot.

Add the Lentils to the sauce pot, bring to a boil and then simmer for 15 minutes.

Add the Peppers and the Spices and simmer until the Lentils are tender.

Taste and adjust the seasoning.

Yield is 2 Quarts.

"Slow Food"

"Slow Food" was the heart of our culinary mission at the Brick Oven Bistro. It is more a philosophy than a cuisine – one that is defined in part by how food is prepared, and how it should be enjoyed.

Slow food is about local ingredients, and traditional cooking methods. We at Brick Oven Bistro were proud to be a part of this movement. Our menu was full of new and innovative ideas to old classics, and everything was made fresh in our kitchen.

Slow Food underscored our belief that part of a good and healthy life consists of sitting down and breaking bread with friends and family, in other words slowing down at mealtime and enjoying!

Seville Black Bean Soup

The inspiration for this soup came from a meal on the coast of Northern California. When we first enjoyed this soup, it was served with grilled sausage and to our taste was delicious. We realized however that the flavors were well suited to recreating it as a vegetarian soup. In the process we renamed the soup for our favorite oranges. Here it is! Consider topping this with chopped Parsley and perhaps a dollop of Sour Cream or Crème Fraiche.

1 TBSP Canola Oil
1 TBSP Cumin
1 ½ tsp Coriander
¾ tsp Cayenne Pepper

2 Cups Yellow Onion, diced
1 Cup Carrots, grated
2 ½ tsp Garlic, minced

2 ½ Lbs Black Beans, soaked overnight and drained
3 TBSP Veggie Base
1 Gallon Water

1 ½ tsp Lemon Juice

2 Oranges – see note about zesting them prior to peeling, seeding and chopping
½ Cup Orange Juice

1 TBSP Oregano
1 ½ tsp Black Pepper
2 tsp Kosher Salt
1 ½ tsp Tabasco
1 ½ tsp Dry Sherry

Soak the Black Beans in a gallon of water and a TBSP of Kosher Salt overnight. Just before cooking, rinse and drain the beans and set aside to add as noted in the recipe.

Zest the 2 Oranges and set the zest aside for use at the end of cooking.

Heat the Canola Oil over medium heat in a large sauce pot. Add the Cumin, Coriander and Cayenne and cook for 1 minute to allow the flavors to release.

Add the Yellow Onion, Carrot and Garlic to the sauce pot and sauté until tender.

Add the Black Beans, Veggie base and Water to the sauce pot.

Add the Lemon Juice, chopped Oranges and Orange juice to the sauce pot.

Add the Oregano, Pepper, Salt, Tabasco and Sherry to the sauce pot and over high heat bring to a boil. Then reduce the heat and simmer until the beans are tender, about 3 hours.

When the beans are tender, taste the soup and add the reserved

Orange zest to heighten the flavor. If it is too acidic for your taste, add Brown Sugar.

Top with a dollop of Sour Cream or Crème Fraiche and Parsley and serve.

Yield is 1 ½ Gallons.

100

Veggie Burgoo

This was our very first all Veggie Soup on our menu, and it remained a popular choice even for Meat-Eaters!

> 1 TBSP Veggie Base
> 2 Qts Water
> 1 Bay Leaf
>
> 1 TBSP Honey
> 1 TBSP Burgundy Wine
> ½ tsp Worcestershire Sauce
>
> 1 tsp Granulated Sugar
> ¼ tsp Marjoram
> ⅛ tsp Basil
> ⅛ tsp Thyme
> ⅛ tsp Black Pepper, coarse grind
> Pinch White Pepper
> Pinch Cayenne Pepper
> ⅛ tsp Green Peppercorns

1 tsp Garlic, minced
½ Cup Red Onions, diced
½ Cup Yellow Onions, diced

½ Cup Cabbage, diced
½ Cup Carrots, half moon
½ Cup Cauliflower, small florets
½ Cup Celery, sliced
½ Cup Green Pepper, diced
½ Cup Mushrooms, sliced
½ Cup Zucchini, half moon
2 Cups Red Potatoes, diced

½ Cup Frozen Corn
½ Cup Roasted Red Pepper, diced

Place the Veggie Base, Water, Bay Leaf, Burgundy Wine and Worcestershire in a sauce pot. Bring to a boil.

Place all the remaining ingredients into the sauce pot and bring back to a boil. As soon as the Red Potatoes are fork tender, turn off the heat.   Yield is 2 Quarts.

Sense of Urgency!

On a video of Thomas Keller's kitchen in Napa, California, we saw this phrase, posted on the wall. "Perfect!" I said. The next morning, it graced ours! Thanks, Thomas!

Sweet Potato Star Anise Soup with Gingered Crème Fraiche

We love sweet potatoes, which make a wonderfully creamy and sweet (duh!) soup...but the idea of using star anise as a flavor counterpoint came from the cookbook, "Hot Sour Salty Sweet: A Culinary Journey Through Southeast Asia", by Jeffrey Alford and his wife, Naomi Duquid. The couple spent months traveling down the Mekong River, collecting cooking ideas and recipes from villages along the way.

For this soup, which we adapted from the intrepid authors who combine their love of food with an interest in anthropology (makes sense to us), we start by cooking star anise with our sweet potatoes -- then we add cream and puree the mixture. We end up with a soup whose creamy sweetness is balanced by the licorice notes of the star anise. But we don't stop there. We add a generous dollop of a ginger-infused creme fraiche before serving. Our creme fraiche is created by letting heavy cream and buttermilk sit over night to essentially become a clotted cream. We then grate fresh ginger into it. When added to the soup, it introduces a sourness that accents the sweetness of the sweet potato, while the star anise and ginger add some delightful complexity to the flavor.

This soup easily becomes vegetarian by using a Veggie Base rather than the Chicken Base. The choice is yours! You have to admit... This sure beats opening a can of chicken noodle soup, doesn't it?

Crème Fraiche:
1 Cup Heavy Cream
2 TBSP Buttermilk

1 TBSP Ginger, peeled & grated

Soup:
5 Lbs Sweet Potato

4 TBSP Butter
1 ½ Cups Yellow Onions, chopped

1 TBSP Ginger, peeled & grated
6 pods Star Anise

2 TBSP Chicken Base or Veggie Base
2 Qts Water

1 Cup Heavy Cream
2 TBSP Triple Sec
¼ tsp White Pepper

Crème Fraiche: At least 24 hours ahead of time combine the Heavy Cream and Buttermilk in a glass or plastic jar, cover and let it sit at room temperature for at least 24 hours, until it is thick. Add the peeled grated Ginger, mix well and place in the refrigerator to cool.

Soup:

Peel and cut the Sweet Potato into 1" pieces. Hold in enough water to cover the sweet potatoes and reserve for use later.

Melt the butter over medium heat in a large sauce pot.

Add the onions and sauté until they are cooked, but not browned.

Add the Ginger, Star Anise and drained Sweet Potatoes to the sauce pot.

Mix the Chicken Base and Water until fully mixed, add to the sauce pot, scraping the bottom well.

Increase the heat and bring to a boil, then simmer for about 20 minutes or until the Sweet Potatoes are completely tender.

Remove the Star Anise pods and using a hand blender or in a blender, blend the soup until smooth.

Return to the sauce pot, add the Heavy Cream, Triple Sec and White Pepper and simmer over medium heat until desired temperature is reached. Taste and adjust seasonings, adding Kosher Salt or more Pepper if desired.

Place a dollop of Crème Fraiche on top of the soup when serving.

Yield is 2 Quarts.

Cookbooks, we Love!

Often when we shared with friends and even family that we would come home and prepare dinner, we were met with a raised eyebrow and the question "Why would you do that? You own a restaurant." Observant comment for sure.

We came home and cooked as we love cooking and we love recipes. Cookbooks to us are like adventure novels to others.

Over the years we have amassed a collection of cookbooks that grace the walls of our living room and spill over into our offices. Looking through them is like taking a very long vacation all over the world. There is hardly a cuisine that is not represented and we have a good sampling of the recipe books of the great chefs.

It seems to be genetic as well. Steph's Mom left binders full of clipped recipes from Philippine newspapers, one sister was a Food Editor, the other creates annual cookbooks, Jeff's uncle and cousin both wrote cookbooks of family favorites. Clearly, a family affair!

For us, cooking is a lifelong love. We hope it will be so for you!

Vichyssoise

Possibly one of the greatest creations ever dreamed up and cooked! As they say "that is my opinion and I could be right!" When asked by staff, "What is this" I was known to respond, "the closest thing to liquid velvet that you will ever taste, rich and luscious!" Well, that drew a raised eyebrow! And yet, there were the fearless, who tried it and loved it. On a warm summer day, we can't imagine anything better!

1 ½ Lbs Idaho Russet Potatoes, peeled and chopped
2 Quarts Water

¼ Lb Butter

1 Large leek, white part only chopped (1 ½ Lbs)
½ Cup Yellow Onions, chopped

1 TBSP Chicken Base
½ Cup Water

3 Cups Potato Water
½ Cup White Wine, dry

3 ½ Cups Whipping Cream
1 ½ Cup Milk

¾ tsp Kosher Salt
¼ tsp White Pepper

Place the Potatoes and the Water in a stock pot over high heat. Bring to a boil and boil for 5 minutes. Reduce the heat and simmer until the Potatoes are soft but not falling apart.

Reserve 3 Cups of the Potato Water for use later. Drain the Potatoes and set aside to use later.

Melt the Butter over medium high heat in a sauce pot. Add the Leeks and the Onion, mix fully with the butter, cover and let braise over low heat for 15 minutes, or until soft.

Dissolve the Chicken Base in the water, then add to the Leek and Onion mix.

Add the reserved Potatoes, Potato Water and White Wine. Using an immersion blender or transferring the sauce pot contents to a blender, blend until smooth.

Place in a bowl in the refrigerator until completely cooled.

When cool, add the Whipping Cream, Milk, Salt and White Pepper. Mix completely.

Taste for seasoning and adjust as desired. Top with chopped chives.

Yield is 2 ¼ Quarts.

Chilled Creamy Tomato Tarragon Soup

We are huge fans of chilled soups. When we introduced them in the restaurant, they met with many a raised eyebrow, "Chilled Soup?!" Our staff graciously offered samples and this soup won over many a skeptical guest. When serving, top this with chopped Basil, Chives, Parsley or Lemon Balm.

108

1 46 oz can V-8 Juice, Chilled
1 ⅓ Cup Sour Cream
⅛ tsp Kosher Salt
¼ tsp Black Pepper
¼ tsp Tarragon

⅓ Cup English Cucumber, peeled and chopped finely

2 Pcs Green Onion, chopped finely

2 tsp Lemon Zest
2 TBSP Lemon Juice

We chilled the V-8 juice to reduce the time from making this soup to serving it. Certainly, you can use a can off the shelf, allowing the time for it all to chill before serving!

Mix completely the V-8 Juice, Sour Cream, Salt, Pepper and Tarragon.

Add the English Cucumber, Green Onion, Lemon Zest and Lemon Juice. Adjust seasonings to taste.

Yield is 2 Quarts.

"If you love a recipe, set it free!"

Louisiana Creole Gumbo

Before the Beanery on 5th and Main opened, Jeff and partner
Ross went to New Orleans in search of food ideas. They were
told to be sure to visit the famous New Orleans restaurant, Dooky
Chase's. Dooky's daughter and current owner, Leah, visited with
them and when she learned that they were opening a restaurant in
Boise, she said "Hon, you gotta have the Gumbo!" Disappearing
into the kitchen and reappearing with Dooky's recipe!

For her, it wasn't about aiding and abetting the competition, it was about the conviction that life is simply too short not to have a place to go for the gumbo that kept Louis Armstrong coming back for more. Somebody say "amen"!

The original recipe included Andouille Sausage. We included it at the beginning, and it was received with concern about the "Heat"! As guests' palates matured, we inched up the heat. In the last years, Jeff made from scratch the Bistro Smoked Andouille Sausage, which we continue to prepare to this day. Our Gumbo was great, hot or not!!

We served this always with a scoop of Veggie Rice (Pg 160) in the centre!

Roux:
1 Cup Flour
¾ Cups Canola Oil

Gumbo:
½ Cup Canola Oil
3 ½ Cups Yellow Onions, diced
4 cloves Garlic, minced
⅓ Jalapeno, minced
(reserve the ribs and seeds to add if you want more heat)

2 ½ Cups Green Pepper, diced
2 ½ Cups Celery, diced

3 Cups Water
2 TBSP Chicken Base

3 Cups V-8 Juice
6 Cups Diced Canned Tomatoes

1 Lb Kielbasa Sausage, sliced into thin ovals
½ Lb Hot Italian or Andouille Sausage, cooked, sliced into thin ovals
¾ Lb Turkey, chopped into ½ inch cubes
¼ Lb Ham, chopped into ½ inch cubes

½ Cup Parsley, chopped
2 Bay Leaves
1 tsp Basil
1 tsp Marjoram
1 ¼ tsp Thyme
1 tsp Black Pepper, coarse grind
½ tsp Cayenne Pepper
½ tsp Kosher Salt
1 tsp Tabasco Sauce
2 tsp Worcestershire Sauce

1 Lb Frozen Okra

Roux preparation: In an oven-proof pan, mix oil and flour and bake at 300 degrees for 20 minutes, until it is the color of sand. Set aside to cool, for later use.

In a large sauce pot, heat the Canola Oil and over medium high heat, sauté the Onions, Garlic and Jalapenos for five minutes.

Add the Celery and the Green Pepper and continue to sauté until crisp tender.

Completely dissolve the Chicken Base into the Water. Add to the Veggies in the sauce pot, along with the V-8 juice and the Tomatoes.

Bring to a boil, constantly checking the bottom of the pot to insure that nothing is sticking!

Using a Whisk, add the room temperature Roux in 4 batches, mixing in thoroughly and allowing the contents to come to a boil between each addition. When thickened, add the remaining ingredients up to the Okra. Bring this to a boil, then reduce the heat and allow this to simmer on the stove for at least an hour. Add the Okra, frozen is fine, and simmer for another 45 minutes.

As with many stews, this one is often best if made a day ahead of time, cooled overnight and reheated the next day!

*"Next to jazz music, there is nothing that lifts
the spirit and strengthens the soul more than a
good bowl of chili."*
Harry James

Chicken & Black Bean Chili

Unlike many of the recipes that we developed over the years,
this recipe is one that we served on opening day and every day
thereafter. It is an iconic Bistro classic! Can you use canned
beans? Of course, you can. Will it taste the same? We'll leave
that to you! We always started our recipes with dried beans, even
though the canned ones would have been perhaps easier. As often
is said in the southern climes of the world:

"El angelito es en las detalles."   The angel is in the details!

Chicken & Black Bean Chili

The day before, combine and store overnight in the refrigerator:
2 Cups Black Beans, dry
1 Gallon of Water
3 TBSP Table Salt

The next day for the beans:

3 Qts cold Water

½ Cup Olive Oil
2 ¾ Cups Yellow Onion, diced
2 ¾ Cups Green Pepper, diced
1 TBSP Garlic, minced
1/3 Cup Chili Powder
⅛ tsp Cinnamon
⅛ tsp Coriander powder
1 TBSP Cumin

½ Cup Masa Harina Flour

1 48 Oz Can V-8 Juice

¼ Cup Chicken Base
1 Cup Hot Water

¼ Cup Honey
⅛ tsp Tabasco
1 ½ tsp Cocoa
1 TBSP Green Peppercorns, chopped
1 ½ tsp Basil
1 ½ tsp Oregano
⅛ tsp Cayenne Pepper
½ tsp Black Pepper
½ tsp White Pepper
1 tsp Kosher Salt

1 ¾ Cups Red Pepper, canned, chopped
1 ¼ Cups Green Chili Peppers, diced

1 ½ Cups Crushed Tomatoes

1 Lb Chicken, cooked and diced

The following day, drain the soaked Black Beans and rinse them very well. Place the beans in a sauce pot add the cold Water and bring to a boil. Once at a boil, reduce the heat and simmer until the Beans are tender. Drain and set aside for use later.

Heat the Olive Oil in a large sauce pot and when hot, add the Vegetables and the Chili Powder, Cinnamon, Coriander and Cumin and sauté over medium high heat until the Onions are translucent and tender.

Add the Masa Harina Flour and sauté for two minutes, stirring continually.

Add the V-8 juice and increase the heat to high. Stir it completely, then allow it to simmer until the mixture thickens.

Add all the remaining ingredients, bring to a boil and then reduce the heat to a simmer and simmer for an hour, stirring occasionally to insure that nothing sticks to the bottom.

Add the cooked, drained beans and simmer for an additional twenty minutes.

As with many stews, this one is often best if made a day ahead of time, cooled overnight and reheated the next day!

❧*Shared Memories*

One of the most memorable visits to the Beanery was many years ago when our kids were aged 4-7. It was during the Christmas holidays. My wife's and my families are from North Idaho. Due to poor roads, they were unable to travel to Boise for the holidays. Since we did not have guests visiting that year, we decided to go to the Beanery for a "special" holiday dinner with the kids. It was snowing in Boise, the streets were bare and the Beanery was open. They all got the big sized milkshakes. It was a great evening. Thanks for being part of our lives. Best,
Jake, Val, Kelly, Julie and Brad Heusinkveld

Chicken or Turkey Mulligatawny Stew

This recipe reminded me of curries from my childhood. Slightly spicy and slightly sweet, these wonderful savory flavors that still remind me of warm breezes and tropical vistas!

Roux:
1 Cup All Purpose Flour
¼ Lb Butter, melted

¼ Cup Olive Oil
¾ tsp Curry Powder
⅛ tsp Cinnamon
½ tsp Kosher Salt
Pinch ground Cloves
Pinch White Pepper

1 Cup Yellow Onions, chopped
1 Cup Carrots, half rounds
½ Cup Celery, chopped

2 Qts Water
¼ Cup Chicken Base

½ Cup Roasted Peeled Red Peppers, chopped
½ Cup Cored Peeled Granny Smith Apple, chopped
2 TBSP Parsley, chopped

¾ Lb Chicken or Turkey, cooked and diced

Roux preparation: In an oven-proof pan, mix melted butter and flour and bake at 300 degrees for 20 minutes, until it is the color of sand. Set aside to cool, for later use.

In a large sauce pot, heat the Olive Oil and over medium high heat, cook the spices for about two minutes until fragrant.

Add the Yellow Onions, Carrots and Celery and continue to sauté until crisp tender.

Completely dissolve the Chicken Base into the Water. Add to the Veggies in the sauce pot, and bring to a boil.

Using a Whisk, add the room temperature Roux in 2 batches, mixing in thoroughly and allowing the contents to come to a boil between each addition.

When thickened add the remaining ingredients. Bring this to a boil, then reduce the heat and allow this to simmer on the stove for at least an hour.   Yield is 2 Quarts.

♧

One of the very nicest things about life is the
way we must regularly stop whatever it is we
are doing and devote our attention to eating.
Luciano Pavarotti

♧

Chicken or Turkey Fricasse

Search for this dish on the internet and you will find recipes in many a cuisine. There are recipes for Cajun, Cuban, French and Old Fashioned Fricasse. It is said that this was Abraham Lincoln's favorite dish, and you can find the recipe attributed to him. Our Fricasse is a pleasure to eat. We hope you will enjoy it as well!

½ tsp Chicken Base
½ Cup Water
6 TBSP Dry Sherry

1 Cup Red Onions, diced
1 Cup Carrots, half moon
1 Qt Mushrooms, sliced
1 Cup Milk
1 Cup Heavy Cream
1 Qt. Corn Gravy Base (Pg 166)

1 tsp Kosher Salt
½ tsp Black Pepper, coarse grind
¾ tsp Thyme
2 TBSP Parsley, minced
1 ¼ Qts Chicken or Turkey, ½ " dice
2 Cups Peas, frozen

Place Chicken Base, Water and Sherry in a stock pot and mix well

to dissolve the Base.

Add the Red Onions, Carrots and Mushrooms to the stock pot. Cover and heat over low temperature for 15 to 20 minutes, until the veggies are crisp tender.

In a large bowl, mix the Milk, Heavy Cream and Corn Gravy Base until smooth.

Add to the stock pot and bring to temperature.

Add the Salt, Pepper, Thyme, Parsley, Chicken and Peas and bring to temperature.
Taste, adjust seasonings as desired. Serve with a scoop of Hand Mashed Potatoes (Pg 157) or as a Pot Pie in a Puff Pastry shell.

Yield is 2 Quarts.

❧ *The Bean Bulletin*

Earlier we spoke of our weekly bulletin. Rain or shine, busy or slow payday came. Our staff received weekly paychecks and weekly bulletins. We took these moments of communication seriously. With so many moving parts, so many staff who worked part time, it was always a challenge to keep everyone on the "same page". We saw our weekly bulletin as our opportunity to do so. It was part of our whole concept of taking the extra step. If we, as owners, didn't, then how could we possibly ask them to?

There were moments of sheer delight, when we would find something just so right for the bulletin. This was one of the best!

We thank the author Thomas Mandrecki, now the owner and chef of Chez Le Commis, Washington, D.C. for giving us permission to share this with you. It speaks our truth.

"Two hands! Two hands!"

"What?"

You have two hands, don't you chef?"

Staring stupidly, a veritable deer in the headlights, I realized what I was being called out for. Just how ridiculous and slow was it to plate a dish using only one hand? Why was my left arm limp and motionless?.................

At Noma and at other top restaurants, anything but striving for complete and total perfection is a disgrace. And to be frank, it is still a disgrace even outside of those top kitchens. The lesson here is just as simple as having a sense of urgency: Don't bother doing anything but your best. Don't half-ass anything. It's either perfect -- or it's not.

Kitchens are so adamant about this fact that the French word, soigné, is to cooks a sacred maxim: "Make it perfect." There are no shortcuts at Noma, and there shouldn't be either when key business decisions are made, or when politicians wrangle in Washington over farm subsidies, or when a college student writes a paper for his Shakespeare class. They are all one and the same. It's not always easy; sometimes the shortcuts we take are almost

unconscious. But we must strive to address these faults and to do better the next time.

Nothing explains this better than Noma's insistence that cooks and stagiers cut their labels. In Copenhagen, you do not rip tape to label a product -- you perfectly square the edges and snip the ends with scissors or a razor blade.

This of course begs the question: Why does cutting tape matter? Isn't the label identical if you rip the tape? Isn't the label temporary? Isn't this whole thing quite silly and absurd and a bit over the top?

I heard another stagier ask a line cook once about the tape issue. The cook's response was crushing: "Because that's a reflection of you."

Cutting tape isn't about the label. It's about arriving earlier and leaving later. It's about leaving as little as possible to chance. It's about always saying, "yes, chef!" -- an affirmation of the fact that nothing is impossible. It's about working harder than the person next to you. It's about never settling. It's an understanding that even when something is an accident or purportedly out of your control, it remains your responsibility.

If we all cut tape, what would the world look like?

As I am writing this, President Barack Obama tweets, "Let us not be trapped by what is. We've got to keep pushing for what ought to be."

"Two hands! Two hands! You have two hands, don't you chef?" Food for thought, indeed.

Thanks Tom!

A page from our Staff Manual

Here are some notions about common courtesy, common sense and the practical applications of the Golden Rule you might want to think about:

1. If you open it, close it.
2. If you turn it on, turn it off.
3. If you unlock it, lock it.
4. If you break it, repair it.
5. If you can't fix it, call in someone who can.
6. If you borrow it, return it.
7. If you use it, take care of it.
8. If you make a mess, clean it up
9. If you drop it, pick it up.
10. If you move it, put it back when you're done.

11. If it belongs to someone else and you want to use it, get permission.
12. If you don't know how to operate it, leave it alone until you learn how.
13. If it doesn't concern you, don't mess with it.
14. If you need help, ask for it.
15. If you say you'll do it, do it.
16. If you say you won't do it, don't.
17. If you can help, offer.
18. If you can't help, stay out of the way.
19. If you don't know what to do, ask.
20. If you know what to do, do it.

Chili Santa Fe

This was the recipe we used when we entered the Chili Cook Off in the early 90's. We did not win "First Place", but we did win a lot of enthusiastic guests asking when we would next serve this, and it kept a favored place in our restaurant!!

¼ Lb Butter

2 tsp Cumin
3 TBSP Chili Powder

1 TBSP Garlic
1 Cup Yellow Onion, diced
1 Cup Green Pepper, diced

3 TBSP Masa Harina

1 ¾ Cups Water

⅔ Cup V-8 Juice
3 TBSP Bistro BBQ Sauce
3 Cups Bistro Rum Sauce pot Beans

1 TBSP Beef Base
¼ Cup Water

½ tsp Basil
½ tsp Oregano
½ tsp Thyme
1 tsp Cocoa
¼ tsp Cayenne Pepper

1 Lb Beef or Pork, Cooked and cut into ½ inch cubes

In a large sauce pot, over medium heat, melt the Butter.

Add the Spices and sauté for 2 minutes.

Add the Onion and Pepper and sauté until tender.
Add the Masa Harina and sauté for 3-4 minutes, do not let it brown.

Add the Water and deglaze the pan, scraping the bottom to release all flavor.

Add all the remaining ingredients and stir well. Bring to a boil and then simmer for an hour. You can also cover the sauce pot with foil and a tight lid and cook in a 300 degree oven for an hour.

Cook or bake until the meat is tender. Taste and adjust seasonings as desired.

Yield is 2 ½ Quarts.

Cowboy Red Eye Stew

One year, we decided to try buffalo. It is most likely that a Ken Burns documentary fueled this decision. Naturally our thoughts on recipes went to West, imagining campfires and campfire stews. Home on the range, what ingredients would they have? Coffee, Whiskey, Buffalo and Potatoes. That was the beginning, the rest follows!

¾ Lb Potatoes, 1" cubes
2 Qts Water

1 TBSP Canola Oil
1½ Lbs Buffalo or Beef Stew Meat, 1" cubes
1 tsp Kosher Salt

⅓ Cup Bourbon Whiskey

⅓ Cup Butter
½ Cup Yellow Onions, chopped
1 ½ tsp Garlic, minced

½ Cup Flour

2 Cups Tomatoes, diced canned
⅓ Cup strong Coffee
2 tsp Worcestershire Sauce

2 tsp Beef Base
3 Cups Water

1 tsp Sage
½ tsp Rosemary
½ tsp Thyme
½ tsp White Pepper
½ tsp Black Pepper
1 tsp Kosher Salt

Place the Potatoes and Water in a sauce pot and bring to a boil. Reduce heat to a simmer and simmer until potatoes are tender, about 10 minutes. Drain and reserve for use later.

Heat the Canola Oil in a sauce pot and sear the meat in batches. Reserve for use later.

Deglaze the sauce pot with the Bourbon and reduce the liquid to 2 Tablespoons.

127

Add the Butter to the sauce pot, once melted, add the onions and Garlic and saute until the onions are soft.

Add the flour, mix well and cook for 5 minutes.

Add the Tomatoes, Coffee, Worcestershire, Beef Base and Water and whisk until all the flour is incorporated.

Add the spices and mix in well.

Place the cooked meat into the sauce pot, cover and simmer until the meat is tender.
Add the Potatoes, bring to temperature. Taste and adjust
seasonings.   Yield is 3 Quarts.

Madagascar Beef Curry

A "soul-soother" stew. Once again the flavors of the southern seas enter into our culinary universe. Inspirations always have come from memories of meals with family and friends in parts far from these lovely environs. Food connects present and past for us in this dish. We hope you will share it with those you love!

128

¼ Cup Canola Oil
½ Cup Green Apples, diced – leave the peel on!
1 Cup Green Peppers, diced
2 Cups Yellow Onions, diced
1 ½ tsp Garlic, minced

2 TBSP Curry Powder
½ TBSP Coriander
4 ½ tsp All Purpose Flour

1 ½ tsp Beef Base
2 ¼ Cups Warm Water

1 Cup + 2 TBSP Red Wine, dry
¼ Cup Lemon Juice, fresh squeezed
1 Can (13.5 oz) Coconut Milk

1 Pc Bay Leaf
¼ tsp Cayenne Pepper
¼ tsp Cloves, ground
½ tsp Ginger, ground
1 ½ tsp White Sugar

½ Banana, chopped
1 Cup Cauliflower florets
1 Cup Carrots, half moon
1 Cup Green Peas, fresh or frozen
1 Cup Zucchini, half moon
1 Cup Raisins, dark
1 Qt Beef, cooked and cubed

Heat the Canola Oil in a sauce pan and add the Apple, Green Peppers, Onion and Garlic. Sauté until the Onion is soft but not browned.

Add the Curry, Coriander and Flour to the sauce pan and cook for another 3 minutes.

Dissolve the Beef Base completely into the water and add to the sauce pan.

Add the Red Wine, Lemon Juice and the Coconut Milk and the Spices to the sauce pan, bring to a boil and then reduce the heat and simmer for 5 minutes.

Add the Banana, Vegetables and Beef to the sauce pan, bring to a boil, then reduce the heat and simmer for at least 1 hour.

Serve with Veggie Rice (Pg 160)

Yield is 2 Quarts.

Creamy Clam Chowder

We tried varying the seafood soups for our Friday lunch special, however this one was the hands-down favorite and became the mainstay for Friday! It has more body than a traditional New England Clam Chowder, and is what we have found to be a Pacific Coast Clam Chowder! The recipe is in two parts. First, the Base is made. This needs to cool overnight. The next day, combine the Base with the Milk and Heavy Cream, bring to temperature over a medium low heat. We served this with a scoop of our Hand-mashed Potatoes (Pg 157) and topped it with chopped Parsley.

Day 1 -

    Roux:
    6 TBSP Butter
    ¾ Cup All Purpose Flour

    Base:
    1 TBSP Clam Base
    3 Cups Water

    2 ½ TBSP Bacon, cooked and chopped in ¼" dice
    ¾ tsp Garlic
    1 Cup Carrots, half rounds
    1 Cup Celery, chopped
    1 Cup Red Onions, chopped

    ½ tsp White Pepper
    ¾ tsp Thyme
    Dash Tabasco

1 Cup Clams
¾ tsp Parsley

Roux:
Melt the butter in a small sauce pan, add the flour and mix
well. Over low to medium heat, cook the roux for ten minutes,
adjusting the temperature of the burner, so that the roux cooks but
does not brown. Set aside to cool for use later.
Mix the Clam Base with the Water fully and add to a sauce pot.

Add the Bacon, Vegetables, and Spices to the sauce pot and bring
it to a boil.

Whisk the Roux into the boiling stock until fully incorporated and
there are no lumps in the mixture.

Reduce the heat and simmer for 5 – 7 minutes stirring constantly.

Add the Clams and the Parsley. Cool overnight.

Yield is 2 Quarts of Base which will make ¾ Gallon of Chowder.
The remainder can be frozen for use on another day.

Day 2: For 6-8 servings use half of the Base.

1 Qt Clam Chowder Base
1 ½ Cups Whole Milk
1 ½ Cups Heavy Cream

In a sauce pot over medium heat, place all the ingredients.
Whisk until smooth and up to temperature. Do not let this boil!

White Bean and Clam Chowder

While most of our guests loved the New England Clam Chowder the best, there were some of us who longed for this Chowder. The flavors are different for sure, but we would suggest, equally as wonderful as the traditional Chowders of the East!

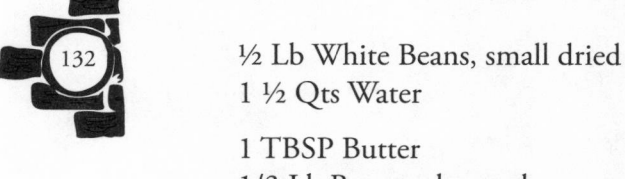
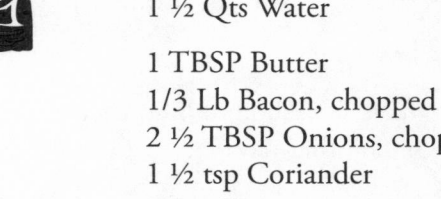

½ Lb White Beans, small dried
1 ½ Qts Water

1 TBSP Butter
1/3 Lb Bacon, chopped
2 ½ TBSP Onions, chopped
1 ½ tsp Coriander
2 tsp Cumin

2 ½ TBSP All Purpose Flour

5 TBSP Clam Broth

½ Cup Clams, drained
1 ½ Cups Corn
½ tsp Black Pepper

1 ¾ Cups Milk
1 ½ Cup Heavy Cream

2 ½ TBSP Cilantro, chopped

Place the White Beans and the Water in a stock pot. Bring to a boil, then reduce the heat to a simmer and simmer until the Beans are tender. Drain them and reserve for use later.

Place the Butter and the chopped Bacon in a sauce pot and sauté for 3 minutes.

Add the Onions, Coriander and Cumin and continue sautéing until the Onions are tender.

Add the Flour to the sauce pot, mix well and sauté for 5 minutes.

Add the Clam Broth to the sauce pot and bring to a boil, stirring constantly.

Add the drained Clams, Corn, Cooked White Beans and Black Pepper and simmer for 10 minutes.

Add the Milk and Cream and simmer until thickened.

Add the Cilantro as you are ready to serve.   Yield is 2 Quarts.

Restaurant Mantra 1

If you can lean, you can clean.

Paradise Pork Stew

Inspired by memories of dinners south, we travel to the Caribbean for the flavors that we highlighted in this stew.

1 TBSP Butter
1 TBSP Canola Oil

1 tsp Kosher Salt
1 ½ Lbs Pork Shoulder, cut into ¾ inch cubes

3 Cups Yellow Onions, chopped
1 TBSP Garlic, minced

⅓ Cup Flour, all purpose

2 tsp Chicken Base
3 Cups Water

1 ½ Cups Apple Cider
1 Cup Dark Beer

2 TBSP Dijon Mustard
1 tsp Coriander
½ tsp Cinnamon
1 tsp Granulated Sugar
½ tsp Kosher Salt
¼ tsp Black Pepper, coarse grind

1 Cup dried Apricots, chopped
1 Cup Prunes, chopped

1 Lb Red Potatoes, peeled and chopped

In a sauce pot over medium heat, melt the butter and then add the Canola Oil.

Sprinkle the Kosher Salt over the Pork cubes. Sear the Pork in the oils, making sure not to crowd the pieces – one layer only. It will need to be done in two or three batches depending on the size of the sauce pot that you are using. As the Pork is seared, remove it to a bowl and continue the process until all the Pork is seared. Reserve for later use.

Add the Onions and the Garlic to the sauce pot and cook until tender, stirring occasionally, about 10 minutes.

Add the flour to the sauce pot and stir, cook for 3 minutes.

Mix the Chicken Base with the Water fully, then add to the sauce pot.

Add the Apple Cider, Dark Beer and the Spices and bring the mixture to a boil.

Add the Apricots, Prunes, Red Potatoes and the Pork to the sauce pot. Reduce the heat and simmer until the Pork is tender.

Taste and adjust seasoning. Serve topped with Citrus Garnish, recipe follows.   Yield is 3 Quarts

Citrus Garnish

2 tsp Lemon Zest
2 tsp Orange Zest
¼ Cup Parsley, minced

Mix fully the Zests with the Parsley. Sprinkle on the top of the Paradise Stew when serving.

Pork Chile Verde

Inspired by wonderful meals in Mexico, a country of many complex cuisines, we were delighted by the number of guests who shared our appreciation for this dish. Use a good piece of Pork Shoulder. We recommend the meats at Meats Royale, a great meat shop with knowledgeable staff and a wonderful selection of meats. Well worth a separate trip!

11 Anaheim Chiles, Whole

¼ Cup Canola Oil

1 tsp Kosher Salt
2 Lbs Pork Shoulder, cut into ¾ inch cubes

¼ Cup Tequila, of good quality

3 Cups Yellow Onions, diced
2 ½ Cups Tomatillos, diced
¼ Cup Garlic, minced

⅓ Cup Masa Harina
4 tsp Cumin
1 ¼ tsp Oregano
1 ¼ tsp Coriander
¾ tsp Kosher Salt

1 TBSP Chicken Base
1 Quart Water

Preheat the oven to 400 degrees.

On a sheet pan, roast the Chiles until the skin is blistering. You can also roast the Chiles over a grill. When well roasted on all sides, place them in a bowl, covered with plastic for at least 10 minutes.
Remove them, peel them, and de-seed and de-rib them, reserving the ribs and seeds in a separate bowl for possible use later.

Chop the peeled Chiles and reserve for use later.

In a sauce pot, over medium high heat, place 2 TBSP of the Canola Oil and heat.

Sprinkle the Kosher Salt over the Pork cubes. Sear the Pork in the Canola Oil, making sure not to crowd the pieces – one layer only. It will need to be done in two or three batches depending on the size of the sauce pot that you are using. As the Pork is seared, remove it to a bowl and continue the process until all the Pork is seared.

When all the Pork is removed from the sauce pot, deglaze it with the Tequila.

Add the Onions, Tomatillos, Garlic, and roasted, peeled Chiles to the sauce pot. Add the seared Pork and any juices that have accumulated in the bowl. Sauté over medium heat until the Onions are soft, about 15 minutes.

Stir in the Masa and the Spices to coat all the ingredients in the sauce pot.

Mix the Chicken Base with the Water fully, then add it to the sauce pot.

Bring all to a boil, then reduce the heat and simmer for at least 45 minutes, or until the meat is tender.

Taste and adjust seasonings. If you prefer it a slightly hotter, add some of the chopped Anaheim seeds and ribs to taste. Serve topped with chopped Cilantro.

Yield is 1 ¾ Quarts.

Wake up and Smell the Coffee!

In 1983, when the restaurant was being created, finding a good cup of coffee in a Boise restaurant was difficult. It was difficult in most of the country, Folgers was the standard.

One of the conversations that Jeff had with his partners was about the ending of too many a dining experience - the flavors of a great meal displaced by a mediocre cup of coffee.

What if you invested in really good coffee?

What if the final memory was of this great coffee?

Thus the decision was made. Finding a quality coffee that was consistent was the next step.

By then, they were in Denver building the Colfax Beanery. Then as now, Denver was a food town. There they found the coffee.

Since 1985. we have purchased our coffee from The Gourmet Coffee Bean, a specialty roaster in Denver. A few years after we began our relationship with them, the company sold to a Nicaraguan coffee grower. The coffee is single bean, single estate coffee, from old vines, which produce rich tasting beans with a chocolate finish.

Delicioso! and Gracias, Carlos y Melva Rondon!

Bistro Pork Pozole

We add to our list of memorable Mexican inspired stews with this Pozole. It can be difficult to find Poblano Peppers in the markets, so we have used Anaheim Peppers instead. This recipe is best made with dried White Beans rather than canned.

1 ½ Cups (½ Lb) large dried Butter Beans (Lima Beans)
2 tsp Kosher Salt
1 Qt Water

½ Lb Poblano Peppers

¾ Lb Pork shoulder, cut into ½ inch cubes

1 TBSP Canola Oil
1 Cup Yellow Onions, chopped
4 tsp Garlic, chopped

½ Lb Tomatillos, skin removed and chopped

2 tsp Chile Powder
2 tsp Cumin
2 tsp Oregano
2 TBSP Pasilla Peppers, chopped

4 tsp Chicken Base
2 Qts Water

2 Cups Hominy

Soak the Beans with the salt overnight in two quarts of water. The next day, rinse and drain them and place them in a sauce pot with another two quarts of water. Bring to a boil and then reduce the heat to a simmer and cook until tender.

Preheat the oven to 400 degrees.

On a sheet pan, roast the Chiles until the skin is blistering. You can also roast the Chiles over a grill. When well roasted on all sides, place them in a bowl, covered with plastic for at least 10 minutes. When cool, remove them, peel them, and de-seed and de-rib them, reserving the ribs and seeds in a separate bowl to make a Poblano paste for use later.

Chop the peeled Chiles and reserve for use later.

In a sauce pot, over medium high heat, heat the Canola Oil.

Sprinkle the Kosher Salt over the Pork cubes. Sear the Pork in the Canola Oil, making sure not to crowd the pieces – one layer only. It will need to be done in two or three batches depending on the size of the sauce pot that you are using. As the Pork is seared, removed it to a bowl and continue the process until complete.

When all the Pork is removed from the sauce pot, add the Onions, Garlic, roasted peeled Chiles to the sauce pot and sauté for approximately 10 minutes.

Once the Onions become translucent, add the Tomatillos and the Spice and cook for another 5 minutes, until the spices release and become fragrant.

Mix the Chicken Base and the Water fully, add to the sauce pot.

Add the seared Pork, Hominy, bring to a boil and then reduce the heat to a simmer. Simmer until the Pork is fork tender.

Add the cooked White Beans and bring to temperature.

Taste and adjust seasonings. If needed add the Poblano Paste.

Yield is 2 Quarts.

142

Poblano Paste

Making this paste allows you to adjust the flavor of the Pozole. This is great to have on hand, it is a great flavor enhancer for salsas and guacamole.

> Poblano Ribs and Seeds, chopped
> 1 tsp White Vinegar
> ½ tsp Salt
> ½ tsp Sugar

In a small bowl, add all ingredients and mix well. Use as noted above!

One can say everything best over a meal.

George Eliot

Shepherd's Stew

Long a favorite of guests, this stew is delicious when made with a variety of meats. We often combined cooked Beef, Pork and Lamb, however it is equally as delicious when made with Lamb alone. At home, we freeze Burgundy Mushroom Gravy and the Base for the Creamy Country Corn Gravy just for the occasion when we want to make this stew! This is one of the stews that we often served as a Pot Pie. If served as a stew, a scoop of Hand Mashed Potatoes (Pg 157) graced the center of the bowl in classic Beanery style!

½ Cup Red Onions, diced
2 Cups Mushrooms, sliced
2 Cups Carrots, half moon
2 Cups Celery, sliced

3 Cups Burgundy Mushroom Gravy (Pg 162)
1 ½ Cups Corn Gravy Base (pg 166)
⅓ Cup Dark Beer

1 tsp Dill
¼ tsp Mint
½ tsp Rosemary
¼ tsp Thyme
1 TBSP Parsley, minced
2 Cups Cooked Meat, ¾ inch cubes
½ Cup Green Peas, fresh or frozen

Steam the veggies until they are crisp tender. Remove them from the heat and set aside.

Place the Burgundy Gravy, Corn Gravy Base and Dark Beer in a large sauce pot.

Add the Spices to the sauce pot and heat to 140 degrees over medium heat.

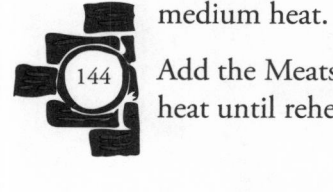

Add the Meats, Green Peas and Veggies and simmer over medium heat until reheated to 140 degrees.   Yield is 2 Quarts.

Our Blog on Pot Pies

As a purveyor of new adventures in comfort food, we'd have to do some heavy penance if we failed to offer pot pie on our menu. I mean, how much more "comfort food" can you get than a meaty pot pie, right?

We do find, however, that some confusion arises among all but the true pot pie connoisseurs when it comes to distinguishing between the "Hunter" and "Shepherd" variations on the pot pie theme. It is, therefore, in the interests of offering a public service that we take a moment to clarify the difference -- a difference that hinges the preference between beer and wine.

Let's start with hunters, why don't we? Here in America, we take it for granted that hunters liked some beers. Our Hunter's Pot Pie, however, has an Old World origin that owes its culinary pedigree more to the Burgundy region of France than to the mountains and woods of America. Our Hunter's Pot Pie is therefore prepared much like a traditional beef bourguignon, and with a noticeable flavoring of mint accompanying the burgundy.

Now, with regards to Shepherd's, we have a much different take on pot pie. Think of the plight of the lonely shepherd, guarding against the depredations of wolf packs crossing the Canadian border to prey on his flocks and, no doubt, take advantage of our health care system. What better way to while away those tedious hours than with a brewski or two? In tribute to these stalwarts, therefore, we add beer to a chicken-based roux. Our Shepherd's Pot Pie has less meat than its Hunter cousin, but with a few beers to accompany it, who the heck is keeping score?

In the case of both pot pie versions, we serve them with fresh baked puff pastry. And speaking of which, we've just added a new item to our menu that you pot pie lovers are going to find very intriguing: our Paradise Pork Stew (Pg 134). Given our penchant for poring over cook books, we recently ran across a recipe that combines potatoes, apple cider, apricots...and ingredients that we can't divulge in the interests of intellectual property protection. Of course, you're free to take a bite and guess all you want.

Hunter's Stew recipe follows!

Hunter's Stew

1 Cup Red Onions, chopped
4 Cups Mushrooms, sliced
4 Cups Carrots, half round
4 Cups Celery, sliced

3 Qts Burgundy Mushroom Gravy (Pg 162)

5 Cups Beef or Beef and Pork, cooked, 1" cubes

1 ½ Cups, Peas frozen
1 ½ Cups, Corn frozen
¼ tsp Green Peppercorns, crushed

¾ tsp Parsley, chopped
¾ tsp Basil
¾ tsp Thyme
¼ tsp White Pepper
¼ tsp Black Pepper

Steam the Vegetables until crisp tender. Set aside for use later.

Place the Burgundy Gravy in a sauce pot and heat to 140 degrees.

Add the remaining ingredients and heat to 140 degrees.

Add the steamed Vegetables and bring back to temperature.

Taste and adjust seasonings.   Yield is 1 Gallon.

"Damn Good" Veggie Stew

Is this title truth in advertising? Indeed, in this case! As one of the more unusual stews that we created, the textures and flavors are wonderful, thus the name!

2 TBSP Dijon Mustard
¼ Cup Olive Oil

1 ½ Cups Yellow Onions
1 Cup Green Peppers, diced
1 ¼ Lbs Red Potatoes, medium dice

2 TBSP Olive Oil
1 ½ tsp Cumin
1 TBSP Chili Powder

1 TBSP Garlic, minced
½ Jalapeno, minced

½ tsp Vegetable Base
½ Cup Water
4 ½ Cups Tomatoes, diced with juice
3 Cups Red Beans, canned, rinsed and drained
¾ Cup Corn, frozen kernels
1 ½ Cup Roasted Red Peppers, diced
1 TBSP Brown Sugar

3 TBSP Dijon Mustard
3 TBSP Sour Cream

Preheat the oven to 425 degrees.

Place the Dijon Mustard and Olive Oil in a large bowl and whisk until smooth and fully incorporated.

Add the Onions, Peppers and Potatoes to the mustard mixture and coat evenly.

Place the coated vegetables in a roasting pan and roast for 30 minutes or until the potatoes are crisp on the outside and tender on the inside. Remove from the oven and reserve for use later.

Place the Olive Oil in a large sauce pot and sauté the Cumin and Chili Powder for about 2 minutes.

Add the Garlic and Jalapeno and continue to sauté for an additional 2 minutes.

Add the Tomatoes, Beans, Corn, Red Peppers and Brown Sugar to the sauce pot, bring to a boil and then simmer for 20 minutes.

Add the reserved roasted Potatoes, Green Peppers and Onions to the sauce pot.

Add the Dijon Mustard and Sour Cream to the sauce pot and bring to temperature.

Taste and adjust seasonings as desired.

Yield is 2 Quarts.

 # Meet You for Supper!
What's For Dinner?

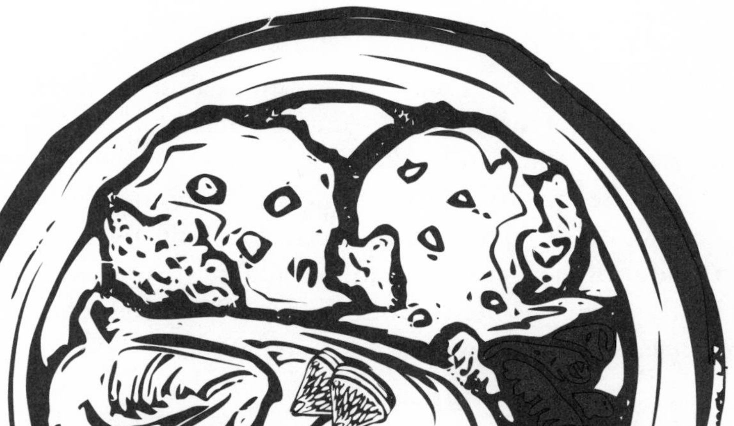

Wild Rice Meatloaf

The truth is that a slice of meatloaf was my favorite breakfast on early mornings at the restaurant! And, it worked for lunch and dinner as well!! When you make this, you will want to use 80/20 Beef, otherwise the final product is too dry. In testing this recipe, we tried two of the wild rice blends available in the markets in town. None of them compared to the wild rice that we used for this recipe which we ordered from Chieftain Wild Rice Company in Spooner, Wisconsin. See our notes on page 73.

150

2 ½ Lbs Ground Beef, 80/20
¾ Lb Ground Pork

3 large Eggs

3 ½ TBSP Whipping Cream
2 tsp Horseradish
2 tsp A-1 Sauce
4 tsp Maggi Seasoning
2 tsp Worcestershire Sauce

1 tsp Garlic
2 ½ TBSP Parsley, freshly chopped

2 tsp Kosher Salt
2 tsp Black Pepper, coarse grind
Pinch Nutmeg, ground
½ tsp Thyme

1 Cup Wild Rice, cooked
1 ⅓ Cups Bread Crumbs
⅓ Cup Soda Water

Crumb the Beef and the Pork into a mixer bowl, to make it easier for them to mix together.

Beat the Eggs in a small bowl and then add to the meat in the mixer bowl.

Add all of the remaining ingredients to the mixer bowl.

Beat until all the ingredients are just mixed together. Do not over beat!

Fill the loaf pan with the Meatloaf, cover with plastic wrap and place in the refrigerator.

It is best to let the Meatloaf rest for at least an hour or overnight before baking.   When ready to bake, let the Meatloaf sit out at room temperature for about thirty minutes.

Bake at 300 degrees until the interior temperature reaches 140 degrees.

Let the meatloaf sit outside of the oven, covered loosely with aluminum foil for about 10 minutes prior to slicing and serving.

Citrus Marinated Chicken

Many a night, we would leave the restaurant for home, stopping in to get ingredients for a new recipe that we had read about. And then, there were the nights when ambition hit the wall of exhaustion. On those nights not much could match our Citrus Chicken for a perfect dinner! This recipe does require some advanced preparation. This chicken is best when it has marinated for 24 to 36 hours. It is a perfect recipe for a party, as all you need to do on the day of the party is remove it from the marinade, dry it and roast it in the oven! It doesn't get much easier or more delicious!!

152

2 Qts Water

¼ Cup Kosher Salt
1 Cup White Granulated Sugar
1 tsp Coarse Black Pepper
1 tsp White Pepper

¾ Cup Lemon Juice
2 TBSP Lime Juice, fresh squeezed
2 6 oz Cans Pineapple Juice
½ Cup Salad Mustard

1 head Garlic, sliced in half – skin on

½ Lemon, sliced in half
½ Lime, sliced in half
½ Orange, sliced in half

6 Skin-on Chicken Halves (Breast, Thigh, Leg)

In a large container that you can lid and store in the refrigerator, place the Water.

Add the Salt, Sugar, Black Pepper and White Pepper and whisk until completely dissolved.

Add the Juices and the Salad Mustard and whisk thoroughly.

Add the Garlic, then squeeze all of the fruit as it is added to the mixture.

Place the Chicken Pieces, skin side down into the mixture so that they are completely covered with liquid. Lid and place in the refrigerator for at least 24 hours, preferably 36 hours.

When ready to roast, remove the chicken from the marinade and dry fully.

Pre–heat the oven to 325 degrees

Place a cookie cooling rack in a baking sheet and spray with a non-stick spray.

Place the Chicken Halves on the rack, skin side up and roast for 30 – 45 minutes until the temperature is 170 degrees.

Depending on your oven, you may want to broil the tops for a few minutes at the end to finish them. Serve with a wedge of lime!

Want to know what the Brick Oven Bistro was all about?

154

Try this little visualization exercise.

It's a warm summer evening in downtown Boise. Children are splashing in the fountain at the Center on the Grove. A live jazz ensemble is playing as a breeze stirs the air and carries with it the scent of the roast citrus marinated chicken. You take a slow, loving sip of an old vine zinfandel that conjures spirits of Beethoven, the Beatles and James Beard as you cozy up to a big bowl of classic New Orleans-style gumbo.

The cacophony of the day fades into the falling waters of the Grove fountain and Lucky, the eternal duck, drops by for a friendly quack and the hope of a couple of crumbs.

Right now you are having "a Brick Oven moment" – not just a meal, but a quiet celebration of the here and now.

Bistro Pot Roast

Over the years, we had several different variations of Pot Roast that we served. What we served was always chosen on the quality and flavor of the final product. We were so delighted when we had Snake River Farms Double R Ranch Beef to use. This recipe was our original and it remains our favorite!

¼ Lb Bacon

3 – 4 Lb Chuck Roast
8 Cloves whole

6 Yellow Onions, sliced thin
1 tsp Thyme
½ tsp Beef Base

Preheat the oven to 325 degrees.

Chop the Bacon into ¼" pieces. Reserve half of the Bacon for use later.

Cut small slits in the surface of the Chuck Roast and into each insert a piece of the Bacon.

Insert the Cloves into 8 of the slits.

Mix the Thyme and the Beef Base with the sliced Onions.

Place the Onions in the bottom of a heavy sauce pot.

Place the reserved Bacon on top of the Onions.

On top of the Onions, place the Chuck Roast. Cover tightly with aluminum foil and then a lid.

Place in the oven. Every thirty minutes, turn the Chuck Roast, rewrap and continue baking. The Pot Roast will be done in 3 ½ to 4 hours.

156

Yield is 4 – 6 servings.

Shared Memories

As Girl Scouts, we always visited the Brick Oven during the Festival of Trees. We worked as volunteers at the festival and having the warm mashed potatoes and gravy helped me stay in the holiday spirits as we helped with festival activities. Thank you for the memories!   Brandy Wiegers

♣

While attending college during the early 1990's I would save my money just to eat at my favorite restaurant, The Beanery, I called it. It was a treat for me. And whenever I wanted to impress out of town company, I brought them to the Beanery! I will miss you.
                                                                Jennifer Swing

Beanery Skin On Hand Mashed Potatoes

We imagine there will be many of you turning to this recipe first!
A few tips – if you need to save on time later in the day, you can
scrub and rinse the potatoes and cut them into chunks early in the
day or even the day before. Then place them in enough cold water
to fully cover them, add 1 tsp of Baking Powder, place them in
the refrigerator. When ready to cook them, drain the water, rinse
them and you will have lovely white potatoes! Every staff person
who worked any length of time for us was involved in making
Mashed Potatoes. It was not unlike a rite of Beanery passage. Do
remember to leave a few chunks of potato, ours were never the
super smooth skin off mashers, nor did we intend them to be!

8 Lbs Idaho Potatoes, washed, scrubbed and cut into
chunks

Water

12 TBSP Butter
1 Cup Buttermilk
1 Cup Milk
2 tsp Kosher Salt
1 tsp Black Pepper, coarse grind

Place the Potatoes in a sauce pot, cover fully with water and bring
to a boil.

Boil the Potatoes until they are beginning to fall apart. Use a slotted spoon and a pair of tongs to check.

When they are ready, immediately drain them.

Place them back in the sauce pot. Add the butter first, mix it in and follow with the remaining ingredients.

Mash them with a hand potato masher. Taste and adjust seasonings as you desire.   Yield is 1 ½ Quarts

Shared Memories

My first taste of what will always be "The Beanery" in my mind, was in 1989 when you were still located on Main Street. Since then I've lived in states from Alaska to Utah and back to Idaho, and every time I return to Boise, I always come back for the "half and half". Your sage nut dressing ruined any other dressing for me, a fact I will never share with my mother. :) No matter the circumstance, I only have to utter the words "corn gravy" to one girlfriend, and it never fails to elicit a smile.

Thank you , thank you, thank you for being willing to share your gift.   Jayne Freeman

Sage Nut Dressing

This recipe changed a bit over the years. At the beginning, we used Rich's Whole Wheat Bread. Then Rich's created the Sunflower Seed Whole Wheat Bread which we loved and changed to. Other than this, you have here our original recipe. This can be made only with French or Italian Bread or you can use half of one of these and half of a Wheat bread. The result will be different. We thought combining the breads resulted in a more interesting texture and flavor.

1 TBSP Vegetable Base
5 Cups Water

1 ½ Cups Celery, sliced
1 Cup Yellow Onions, diced

2 tsp Poultry Seasoning
2 tsp Sage Seasoning
1 ½ tsp Thyme
½ tsp Black Pepper, coarse grind

¾ Lb French or Italian Bread, Cubed
¾ Lb Wheat Bread, Cubed
2 tsp Walnuts, chopped

Place the Vegetable Base and the Water in a stock pot.

Add the Celery, Onions and the Spices and bring to a boil. Reduce to a simmer.

Simmer until the Celery and the Onions are tender.

Add the Bread Cubes and the Walnuts.

Mash to perfection using a hand potato masher.

Yield is 2 Quarts.

Veggie Rice

We used a Parboiled Rice for this recipe. Uncle Ben's Converted Rice works perfectly. In researching rice, we learned that both Parboiled and Converted Rice are soaked and steamed while being processed and in this retain much more of the nutrients than plain rice. We know that this simply tastes good.

2 TBSP Butter
⅓ Cup Celery, sliced
⅓ Cup Carrots, half moon
⅓ Cup Green Peppers, diced
⅓ Cup Yellow Onions, diced
1 ½ tsp Garlic, minced
¾ tsp Black Pepper, coarse grind

1 ½ Cups Uncle Ben's Converted Rice

2 tsp Vegetable Base
3 ⅓ Cups Water

Place the Butter in a sauce pot and melt over medium heat.

Add the Vegetables and the Spices and sauté until crisp tender.

Add the Rice to the sauce pot and sauté for 2 minutes.

Mix the Vegetable Base into the Water until completely dissolved.

Add to the Vegetables and the Rice in the sauce pot.

Bring to a boil. Reduce the heat to a low simmer, cover and cook for 20 minutes.

Remove from the heat. Leave the cover on for an additional 10 minutes. Using a fork, to loosen the Rice prior to serving.

Yield is 1 ½ Quarts.

♣ *Shared Memories*

We had family visiting us from Germany some time back. The Brick Oven Bistro was the first place we could think to take them to eat to get some great home cooking. I think we ordered about every side that was on the menu. They loved every bite and still talk about their visit.   Jim & Jan Justice

Burgundy Mushroom Gravy

In our 2010 blog on this favorite, we wrote about one of our guests whose love for our gravy was legendary! "When Nate of Burlington, Washington comes to visit his in-laws in Boise, he tries to time his arrival for lunch -- which means a straight shot down Vista Avenue from the airport to downtown...and the Brick Oven Bistro. His lunch of choice: Yankee Pot Roast. For Nate, it's all about the gravy. For his wife, Erin, it's all about concealing her identity as her hubby makes his way back to the kitchen for an extra bowl...or three...of the brown nectar.

"It would be embarrassing if it weren't for the fact that he's so cute about asking for more," Erin blushes. "He actually wanted to buy a container to freeze and take back home with us. It makes me feel a bit inadequate as a cook."

What is it that could excite such passion over what for many restaurants is not much more than an afterthought? If you have to ask that question, you've most likely never experienced our famous burgundy mushroom gravy. If you want to know the secret behind it, let's just say that at no point in the process is a can opener involved.

Like everything else at the Brick Oven Bistro, our gravy is slow cooked from scratch. At the risk of over stimulating your taste buds, here's how we do it.

We begin by making a reduction with burgundy wine (surprise) and mushrooms (surprise again!). We then add to this a demi-glace, which for the culinarily challenged among you is a thick, rich beef sauce. As if this weren't enough, we apply a traditional French finish of brandy and butter. We know this sounds decadent, but if you're really that calorie conscious you should probably just stick with a salad.

So...why go through all this effort if we could just open a can? The simple answer is that Nate would never forgive us if we did. Besides, there is significant symbolism in the way we make our gravy. After all, lavishing this much attention to what goes on our food speaks volumes about what goes into it."

4 Bay Leaves
5 Cups Mushrooms, sliced
1 ½ Cups Yellow Onions, diced
½ tsp Garlic, minced
⅛ tsp White Pepper
1 Qt Red Wine, dry

9 Oz Demi Glace base
2 Qts Water

3 TBSP + 1 tsp Brandy
12 TBSP Butter

Place the Bay Leaves, Mushrooms, Yellow Onions, Garlic, White Pepper and Red Wine in a stock pot. Bring to a boil and reduce by a third. Set aside for use later.

Trick: Place a chopstick in the stock pot. It will leave the red wine mark on it, which is your original amount. It is then easy to mark it for the level you are reaching and to use this as your guide, so that you do not under or over reduce the amount.

Place the water and the Demi Glace base in a separate stock pot.

Whisk fully and bring to a boil

Reduce the heat to a simmer and allow this to thicken for 20 minutes. This mixture will fully coat a spoon when it has reached the proper thickness.

Add the Wine reduction to the thickened Demi Glace sauce.

Add the Brandy to the gravy, whisk in well.

Cut the Butter into tablespoons and add one at a time whisking fully between each addition.   Yield is 3 ½ Quarts.

When I heard you were closing your doors, I was in shock. My favorite restaurant of ALL TIME couldn't be leaving!

When we moved to the Treasure Valley in the early 90's, we didn't know any good restaurants. We had 5 children, so cost and friendly atmosphere were very important. When we found the Beanery, we were in love. It had everything we were looking for, plus the BEST food! It was everyone's favorite, hands down. Cafeteria style worked so well with kids! When we had a birthday, that's where we went for our Bistro Birthday dinner gift.

When out of town guests arrived, we went straight to the Beanery. And when you changed your name to the Bistro, we still loved you.

Our kids are now grown, but we will always have our great memories of going to your wonderful restaurant. Getting the red star on our receipt was the jackpot prize to beat them all! Your mashed potatoes with corn gravy, sage dressing, and cranberry sauce were my personal favorites. Didn't matter what I put with them (turkey, meatloaf, citrus chicken, etc) it made it soooo delicious.

Can't wait for the cookbook!!! If you ever get the idea of starting another eatery, DO IT!!!   Lori Thornton

Creamy Country Corn Gravy

Guests wax rhapsodic over this Gravy, which is deceptively simple and a two day process!

Corn Gravy Day 1

Roux:
¼ Lb Butter
1 Cup All Purpose Flour

1 ½ TBSP Vegetable Base
6 Cups Water
½ tsp Thyme
½ tsp Black Pepper, coarse grind

Roux preparation: Two ways to make a Roux.
In an oven-proof pan, mix melted butter and flour and bake at 300 degrees for 20 minutes, until it is the color of sand. Set aside to cool, for later use.

OR

Melt the butter in a small sauce pan, add the flour and mix well. Over low to medium heat, cook the roux for ten minutes, adjusting the temperature of the burner, so that the roux cooks but does not brown. Set aside to cool, for use later.

Place the Vegetable Base, Water, Thyme and Black Pepper in a stock pot and bring to a boil.

Add the cooled Roux, a little at a time, whisking fully between each addition.

When complete with the addition of the Roux and the mixture is smooth without any lumps, reduce the heat and simmer for 10 minutes.

Remove from the stove, place in the refrigerator to fully cool. Do not use this base unless it is completely cooled. Yield is 6 Cups.

Corn Gravy Day 2

> 2 Cups Corn Gravy Base, cold
> 2 Cups Heavy Cream
> ½ Cup Corn kernels

Place the Corn Gravy Base and the Heavy Cream in a large bowl and whisk until completely smooth.

Transfer the Gravy to a Sauce pot.

Add the Corn kernels and mix in well.

Over medium heat, bring to temperature. Yield is 1 Quart.

Cooking is like love. It should be entered into with abandon or not at all.

Harriet Van Horn

Southern Style Gravy

If the thought "Put mo' South in yo' mouth" has been on your mind lately, we offer this. We departed from the traditional sausage most often seen in a Creamy Southern Gravy and created our own slightly spicy Turkey Sausage - our efforts to lighten it up a bit! This gravy is delicious on an Open Faced Ham or Turkey Sandwich and great too on a dinner.

Turkey Sausage:
1 Lb Ground Turkey
1 oz Water, iced
½ tsp Coriander
1 ¼ tsp Kosher Salt
1 tsp Fennel, ground
1 tsp Black Pepper, coarse grind

Place all ingredients in a large bowl and mix well with your hands. This recipe makes enough for two batches of gravy. Freeze half for another day!

Gravy:
1 TBSP Canola Oil
½ Lb Turkey Sausage

1 Quart Corn Gravy Base (Pg 166)
1 Quart Heavy Cream

1 Cup Bacon, cooked and chopped into bits

Place the Canola Oil and the Turkey Sausage in a large sauce pan. Cook until browned. Break up the sausage as it cooks into small chunks. Set aside to add later.

Place the Corn Gravy Base and the Heavy Cream in a sauce pot over medium low heat. Bring to temperature (140 degrees). Add the cooked Turkey sausage. Taste for seasoning and adjust as desired. Top with Bacon Bits! Yield is 2 Quarts.

♣ *Our Staff*

At the heart of downtown, many found home! This book could as well have been titled, Four Thousand Folks later, as when we counted up our staff, that's how many souls we hired! Our staff was our extended family and like proud parents, we wanted our "kids" to benefit from the skills and life lessons working in our restaurant provided them. Delightedly over the years, many returned to share with us their next adventures and we were honored they did!

Thank you for giving me the chance to work for you guys. I learned so much from working in front and when I got to work in the back as the cold prep cook. Many things I use daily. My

favorite is keeping things neat and looking great all the time, as you may never know when someone will walk in the back and you want the best to always to show...along with the use of the word towel and not a rag and how much better things taste made from scratch. Much love and thanks always. Marci L. Serrano De Luna.

I worked in the back and at the take-out window in the mid 90's. I now live in Saint Paul and still make the same mashed potatoes I used to make in huge batches way back then. I miss the spicy cherry sauce terribly and I was saddened to hear that I may never get a chance to taste it again. Working there helped define me. Thank you for those years. Miss you guys. Tim Knox

I just read the news of your plans to close. I worked for you, if I remember correctly, from 2001-2002. Learning the various positions, cemented in me, my interests in all things culinary. Thanks again, Gabe Border

Thanks for being a great second job. It was a fun place to work and meet friends - friends for life. Many people who made a difference in my live I met while working at the Beanery. Best wishes and much happiness. Connie Hopkins Whitmarsh

❧ Shared Memories

Every ten days or so, Linda would say, "I can't think of a thing to cook. Let's go out to dinner tonight." My suggestion was always the Brick Oven Bistro and my favorite dinner, Wild Rice Meatloaf, always comforting, always predictable, always satisfying.

Then there is the warm, welcoming atmosphere of the Bistro and the eclectic young workers with their smiles, earrings, and funny hats.

And you never forgot our birthdays. I have one of your birthday cards on the kitchen table right now. We'll see you one last time this week to use this annual gift of goodness, but from now on, I'll not be celebrating any more birthdays. It just won't be the same without the Bistro.

171

Our best to you as you move on and thanks for so many years of great food. Dick and Linda Miller

❧ And back to you!

To everyone who wrote and shared their thoughts and stories with us, thank you! We will miss being part of all the birthdays. Your enthusiasm enriched our lives. It really won't be the same, for us as well. We treasure our memories. We feel lucky that we were able to do something for others while doing what we love, cooking and entertaining!

 # Today's Special!

172

Red Beans and Rice

Our website blog in April, 2010 was devoted to this dish and read:

"You might think that the demands of running a restaurant for 25 years (make that 26) might detract from the joy of cooking, or that perhaps one's zeal for great food could become somewhat muted. That could easily be the case, except for one thing: among the customers we serve every day there are some pretty remarkable cooks; and interacting with them helps keep our passion alive. Cooking for people that love to cook is like being a "musician's musician" – if you can please them, you know you're on the right track. And every now and then, they return the compliment by inspiring us.

Take Justin Boggs, for example. It turns out that Justin, who is a construction management student at Boise State University by day, has been relentlessly pursuing the ultimate red beans and rice recipe.

We've been cooking red beans and rice for years, and as tradition warrants, it has been a part of our Monday menu – Monday being "washing day" according to regional custom.

Several weeks ago, while we talked about the chefs and recipes that have most influenced our approach to the cuisine of Louisiana, Justin revealed that his grail quest had led him to make his own andouille sausage. It turns out that nothing he had found

commercially available quite nailed the flavor he was searching for. We have to admit that he seemed slightly obsessed, but to

paraphrase Barry Goldwater, "extremism in the defense of culinary authenticity is no vice." We ended our conversation by inviting Justin back to the restaurant to share his recipe with us, once he felt he had achieved his goal.

We knew Justin was making progress when he posted a story on a local food blog, "Mundovore: Eat the World", detailing his adventures in making his andouille sausage from scratch. You have to give it to the man…he's a machine. We sensed that a reunion would not be long away.

The other day Justin came by with a container of the fruits of his labor. We took it back to the kitchen, heated it up, and brought out a bowl of our own rice to serve with it.

Now, before I go any further with this tale, let me make something clear. We're not food snobs – but we've been around the culinary block a time or two, and we've had some damn good food over the years -- some of it we've cooked, and much of what we've learned has gone into our menu. But Justin's red beans and rice, particularly his homemade sausage, raised the bar for us when it comes to this traditional favorite. In a word, we were blown away.

By the time we "licked the platter clean," we were working out a deal with Justin to provide him with 20 pounds of pork for his next run of andouille sausage…in return for some of the final product. Who knows…we might share some of it with the rest of

you. Consider it our way of saying thanks for not only bringing us
your business, but your inspiration
as well. To all the Justins out there,
we salute you! "

Justin inspired Jeff to make our
own andouille! There are gifts in
collaboration! And here are the
Red Beans for you!!

The day before:
¾ Lb or 1 ¾ Cups Red
Beans, dry
1 Gallon of Water
3 TBSP Table Salt

1 Ham Hock

3 Qt. Cold Water

1 TBSP Chicken Base
1 TBSP Beef Base
⅔ Cup Hot Water

¾ tsp Tabasco
2 TBSP Worcestershire Sauce

⅛ tsp Black Pepper, coarse grind
Pinch Cayenne Pepper
Pinch White Pepper

Pinch Cloves, ground
½ tsp Oregano
½ tsp Thyme
¾ Cup Celery, diced
¾ Cup Green Peppers, diced
¾ Cup Yellow Onions, diced
¾ tsp Garlic, minced

¾ Cup Ham, chopped
2 oz Andouille Sausage, cut into half moons

The day before making this recipe, place the dry Red Beans in a container with the Water and Salt. Cover and place in the refrigerator to soak.

The following day, drain the soaked Red Beans and rinse them very well. Place the beans in a large sauce pot.

Soak the Ham Hock in enough milk to cover, for 30 minutes, then rinse and place in the sauce pot with the Red Beans.

Add the cold Water to the sauce pot.

Mix the Chicken Base and Beef Base with the hot Water and dissolve completely. Add to the sauce pot.

Add the Tabasco and Worcestershire to the sauce pot.

Add the spices to the sauce pot. Over high heat, bring this to a boil, then simmer until the beans are barely tender.

Once the beans are barely tender add the vegetables to the sauce pot and continue simmering for another 40 minutes.

Add the Ham and the Andouille Sausage to the sauce pot and continue simmering, until the liquid has thickened. On a very low heat, this can cook for many hours.

Before serving, remove the Ham Hock from the Red Beans. Dice any Ham that you remove from the Ham Hock and return it to the Red Beans.   Yield is 2 Quarts.

Kielbasa Sausage for Red Beans

Slice the Kielbasa Sausage, on a diagonal, into 1 inch thick slices. Place in a sauce pot of gently simmering water to heat up. To add flavor, add some dark beer to the water.
Top the Red Beans with Veggie Rice (Pg160) and 2 Kielbasa Sausage pieces.

♧Showtime!!

To get the real feel of the moment of restaurant doors opening, watch "All That Jazz", the film of Bob Fosse.
Imagine 6am on a Saturday morning. Artists and Farmers are slowly setting up their booths for the Market. Produce deliveries are coming, the ovens are warming up, the patio flowers being watered, dining room floors swept, specials boards written up, prep list for the day posted, ice bins being filled. Staff arrive, the preparation continues. 9am   Doors Open...It's Showtime!

Wednesday: Kobe Meat & Cheese Roulade

Snake River Farms American Kobe Beef, in a word, divine! We had made this Roulade for many years using ground beef, once we tried it with the Kobe, there was no turning back. The great treat on Wednesdays was to be the staff person who received a taste of the end piece – it made the day!

    1 ½ Cups Bread Crumbs
    2 lbs Snake River Farms ground Kobe Beef

    4 large Eggs
    1 ½ tsp Maggi Seasoning

    1 ½ tsp Kosher Salt
    1 ¼ tsp Black Pepper, coarse grind
    1 ½ tsp Oregano
    1 ½ tsp Garlic Powder

    Filling:
    1 Cup Kielbasa Sausage, diced
    1 Cup Swiss Cheese, shredded   (you can use instead a
    Provolone/Mozzarella mix)

Crumb the Beef into a mixer bowl and add the Bread Crumbs.

Beat the Eggs and Maggi in a small bowl and then add to the mixer bowl.

Add the spices to the mixer bowl. Beat until all the ingredients are just mixed together. Do not over mix!

One rolls this just as one would make a jellyroll. It is easiest to use parchment paper.

Place this Kobe mixture on top of a sheet of parchment paper, which you have lightly sprayed with canola oil spray.

Place another oiled sheet on top of the meat and using a rolling pin, roll out evenly until about ¼" inch thick.

Leaving a 1 ½" space around three sides, sprinkle the diced Kielbasa and Cheese on top of the meat. Using the paper to guide you, roll the meat tightly. Pinch the edges and lay the seam side down on the baking pan. Cover with plastic wrap and refrigerate.

It is best to let the Roulade rest for at least an hour or overnight before baking. When ready to bake, let the Roulade sit out at room temperature for about thirty minutes.

Bake at 300 degrees until the interior temperature reaches 140 degrees.

Rest the Roulade outside of the oven, covered loosely with aluminum foil for about 10 minutes prior to slicing and serving.

Yield is 6 large servings.

Egg Noodle Suppers

Beef Stroganoff, Hungarian Goulash and Chicken or Turkey Tetrazzini became the stews that we served on Egg Noodles as a Supper Special. Certainly any of these could be served as a stew with Hand Mashed Potatoes in the center, however we think each of these is even tastier when placed on top of Egg Noodles. We hope you will give these a try!

Beef Stroganoff

2 tsp Butter
1 Cup Yellow Onions, chopped
¾ tsp Garlic, minced

1 TBSP Brandy

1 ½ Lbs Ground Beef

1 ½ Qts Burgundy Mushroom Gravy (Pg 162)
2 TBSP Worcestershire Sauce
½ Cup Red Wine
⅔ Cup Sour Cream

1 ½ Cups Mushrooms, sliced

Place the Butter in a sauce pan and melt. Add the Yellow Onions and Garlic and sauté until the Onions are slightly golden.

Add the Brandy, flambé if you know how to do so safely, otherwise bring to a boil until nearly all of the Brandy has been cooked off. Place in a bowl and reserve for later.

In the same sauce pan, sauté the Ground Beef until it is cooked. Set aside for use later.

Place the Burgundy Mushroom Gravy, Worcestershire Sauce, Red Wine and Sour Cream in a stock pot and whisk well. Over medium heat bring to temperature (140 degrees).

Add the Mushrooms, cooked Ground Beef, and cooked Onions and Garlic, bring back to temperature.   Yield is 2 Quarts.

❧ *Shared Memories*

This is the quintessential "Secret Local Place" that I am forever searching for when I travel. One cannot live entirely on 5 star $100 dining experiences when traveling, so I make a point to ferret out home-spun comfort food places to supplement when another "hot new" food adventure would send me into digestive coma. The Brick Oven Bistro puts out simple scratch-made American cuisine that your grandmother would have served and then throws the unexpected at you, like Kobe Meat and Cheese Roll and Sweet Potato Soup with Star Anise and Gingered Creme Fraiche. I could go on, but my words would not do it justice. And, I also like where these people are coming from, "We like our food slow cooked, not our planet" a slogan imparted on one of their menu boards.   Ira N. review on Trip Advisor

Hungarian Goulash

2 TBSP Caraway Seeds

1 TBSP Canola Oil
1 ½ Lbs Ground Beef or Stew Meat

1 TBSP Canola Oil
1 TBSP Tomato Paste

3 Cups Yellow Onions, diced
1 ½ TBSP Garlic, minced
3 TBSP Paprika

2 TBSP Beef Base
2 Qts Water

¾ tsp White Vinegar
1 Qt. Tomatoes, diced with juice
1 ½ Cups Roasted Red Peppers, diced

Dash Cayenne Pepper
¼ tsp Black Pepper
¼ tsp White Pepper
1 tsp Marjoram

Place the Caraway Seeds in a small sauce pan and lightly toast them over medium heat. Be careful not to burn them! When cool, grind them and reserve for use later.

Heat the Canola Oil in a sauce pan, add the Ground Beef or Stew Meat and sauté.   When cooked, place in a bowl and reserve for use later.

In a sauce pot, heat the additional TBSP Canola Oil, add the Tomato Paste and cook over medium heat for two minutes.

Add the Onions, Garlic and Paprika and sauté until the Onions are tender.

Dissolve the Beef Base fully in the water. Add to the sauce pot.

Add the remaining ingredients and bring to a boil over medium heat, then reduce the heat to a simmer.

Add the reserved Beef and toasted ground Caraway, simmer partially covered for an hour.   Yield is 2 Quarts.

♣

Tell me what you eat, I'll tell you who you are.

Anthelme Brillat-Savarin

♣

Chicken or Turkey Tetrazzini

Roux:
¼ Cup Butter
¼ Cup All Purpose Flour

3 TBSP Butter
4 Qts Mushrooms, sliced

1 ½ tsp Chicken Base
2 Cups Water

¾ Cup Heavy Cream
1 Cup Milk
¼ Cup Sherry
¼ tsp White Pepper
⅓ Cup Parmesan Cheese

¾ Lb Chicken or Turkey, cooked and julienned
1 ½ Cups Green Peas

Roux:
Melt the butter in a small sauce pan, add the flour and mix
well. Over low to medium heat, cook the roux for ten minutes,
adjusting the temperature of the burner, so that the roux cooks but
does not brown. Set aside to cool for use later.

In a sauce pan, melt the Butter. Add the Mushrooms and sauté over medium heat until the Mushrooms are golden. Set aside for use later.

Mix the Chicken Base with the Water fully and add to a sauce pot.

Add the Cream, Milk, Sherry, Pepper to the sauce pot. Mix until creamy and smooth. Bring to a boil over medium heat.

Whisk the Roux into the sauce pot until fully incorporated and there are no lumps in the mixture.

Add the Parmesan Cheese, Chicken or Turkey and Green Peas to the sauce pot. Heat over medium heat to 140 degrees.

Reduce the heat and simmer for 5 – 7 minutes stirring constantly.

Yield is 1 ½ Quarts

If food is poetry, is not poetry also food?

Joyce Carol Oates

Turkey Meatloaf with Tomato Jam

At home, we have a collection of meatloaf recipes, we love meatloaf! This recipe is a particular favorite that we brought into the restaurant. It is great both warm and cold!

Tomato jam:
¾ Cup Tomatoes, fresh chopped
1 TBSP Olive Oil
2 TBSP Yellow Onions, minced
1 ½ tsp Tomato Paste
1 ½ tsp Granulated Sugar
⅛ tsp Mace
½ tsp Kosher Salt
6 TBSP Ketchup

Meatloaf:
1 ½ Cups Yellow Onions, chopped
1 TBSP Olive Oil
1 tsp Kosher Salt
½ tsp Black Pepper, coarse grind
¼ tsp Thyme

2 ½ tsp Worcestershire Sauce
¾ Cups Chicken Stock
1 ½ tsp Tomato Paste

2 ½ Lbs Ground Turkey
¾ Cup Bread Crumbs
2 Eggs, Large beaten

Tomato jam:
Place the fresh or canned tomatoes in a food processor and pulse until finely chopped. Reserve for use later.

Place the Olive Oil in a sauce pan and heat over medium heat.

Add the Onions and sauté for 1 minutes

Add the Tomato paste and Saute for 1 minutes.

Add the reserved Tomatoes, bring to a simmer. Simmer for 10 minutes until thickened. Add the Ketchup and reserve for use later.

Pre heat the oven to 350 degrees.

Meatloaf:
Place the Olive Oil, Onions, Salt, Pepper and Thyme in a sauté pan and sauté for 15 minutes until the Onions are translucent.

Add the Worcestershire Sauce, Chicken Stock and Tomato Paste and mix well. Cool to room temperature.

Place the Ground Turkey, Bread Crumbs, Eggs and the cooled Onion Mixture in a large bowl. Mix carefully.

Place in greased loaf pan or create a rectangular shape on a sheet pan.

Top with the Tomato Jam.

Place in the oven and bake until temperature is 160 degrees.

Yield is 6 servings.

Meatloaf Ideas

What follows is the short list of some of our favorite meat loaves. Some we have found in Fine Cooking and Saveur Magazines.

Thai Turkey Meatloaf with Green Curry Sauce

Pesto topped Turkey Meatloaf

Turkey, Fennel and Bacon Meatloaf

Indian Spiced Lamb Meatloaf

Sausage Meatloaf with Lemon and Parmesan

Stout and Cheddar Meatloaf

Blue Cheese and Bacon Meatloaf

Spicy Southwestern Meatloaf

Family Dining

The Brick Oven Bistro never consciously set out to be a "family restaurant" per se, but we did very much want to create a family dining experience. We carried this intention through on a lot of levels…but the fundamentals were a casual ambiance, wholesome food, and a staff that embodies the caring that we believe family dinners should model.

Most people who came and ate with us got this intention right from the get-go. You all walked up together and got your food from the people who served it. You interacted with them. You went and sat down together in areas that look like a family dining room. You ate simple, healthy and abundant meals that could just as easily had been prepared by your mother or grandmother. And then you did the most important thing aside from nourishing your bodies. You talked. No distractions. No TV. No one jumping up and running to the kitchen to grab something they'd forgotten (that's what our staff is for!). You just plain "visit."

Alaskan Salmon Loaf with Creamy Green Pea Gravy

Friday's special for decades. Prepared on Thursdays and baked on Fridays, Salmon Loaf was what was always for lunch or dinner for us on those days. Amusingly, part of our staff training was the scripting of the words "Creamy Green Pea Gravy", after we watched a new guest do a double take when told, and it comes with "Pea Gravy". Another of the many opportunities we found to improve communication clarity!

190

> 4 Lbs Salmon, canned and deboned
> 1 ¾ Qts Bread Crumbs
> 1 ¾ Cups Celery, diced fine
> ½ tsp White Pepper
> 1 ½ TBSP Lemon Juice
>
> ½ tsp Anchovy Paste
> ½ Cup Water
>
> 4 Eggs, large
> 1 ¾ Cups Milk
> 1 ¾ Cups Heavy Cream

Spray a 9" x 12" baking dish with a Canola Spray.

Place the deboned Salmon in a large bowl.

Add the Bread Crumbs, Celery, Pepper and Lemon Juice. Toss lightly.

In a separate bowl, whisk the Anchovy Paste and Water until completely mixed.

Add the Eggs, Milk and Heavy Cream to the Anchovy Paste and Water and whisk well.

Add to the Salmon Mix and mix well but gently, preserving some chunks of Salmon.

Place in the prepared baking dish, cover with plastic wrap and refrigerate overnight.

The next day, remove from the refrigerator and allow to sit out at room temperature while you preheat the oven to 315 degrees. Bake for 45 – 55 minutes.   Yield is 8 – 10 servings.

Creamy Green Pea Gravy

2 Cups Corn Gravy Base (Pg 166)
2 Cups Heavy Cream
¼ Cup + 1 TBSP Dry Vermouth

1 Cup Green Peas, frozen or fresh

Place the Base, Cream and Vermouth in a sauce pot and over medium heat bring to a simmer.

Add the Peas, bring back to temperature. Serve!

Yield is 1 Quart.

Saturday: Bistro Lamb Shanks

Our winter Saturday night Comfort Food Classic was often our Bistro Lamb Shank. We slowly braised the shanks in our oven until the meat was falling-off-the-bone tender serving the shank on our Veggie Rice, topped with Burgundy Mushroom gravy. We both love lamb and we were delighted when we found all natural and organic Lava Lakes Lamb, locally produced and delicious! We encourage you to go to their website and order. Often you can find Lava Lakes products as well at the downtown Saturday market.

4-6 Lamb Shanks

1 ½ TBSP Roasted Garlic Powder
1 TBSP Onion Powder
2 ½ TBSP Black Pepper, coarse grind
1 ½ tsp Kosher Salt
1 ½ tsp Thyme

3 Bay Leaves
1 TBSP Rosemary
2 tsp Garlic, freshly chopped
1 Cup Yellow Onions, chopped

2 TBSP Chicken Base
¾ Cup hot Water
1 Cup Red Wine

Preheat the oven to 375 degrees.

Rinse and dry the Lamb Shanks.

Mix the spices, Garlic Pepper through the Thyme, together in a small bowl.

Rub the spice mixture into the Lamb Shanks and place the Shanks in a baking pan large enough so they are in one layer.

Dissolve the Chicken Base in the hot Water in a small bowl.

Add the Red Wine to the Chicken Base and Water and mix thoroughly.

Pour over the Lamb Shanks. Add additional water so that half of the shake is in liquid.

Cover tightly with Aluminum foil and cook covered for 1 hour.

Remove the foil, turn the shanks, re-cover with foil and cook for an additional 1 ½ hours.

Remove the foil, turn the shanks and cook uncovered for an additional 1 hour or until the meat is nearly falling off the bone.

Serve one lamb shank on a bed of Veggie Rice (Pg 160), as we did at the restaurant or on a bed of Hand Mashed Potatoes (Pg 157), topped with Burgundy Mushroom Gravy (Pg 162).

Paco Sanchez's "Super Good" Pork Shank Supper

Good Heavens! We were thrilled when we got the Kurobuta Pork Shanks from Snake River Farms. The challenge was to create a dish that enhanced the great Pork flavors. Jeff invented this dish, gathering inspiration from many a source. He was well thanked by everyone who tasted it – as it is divine!

6 Kurobuta Pork Shanks
2 tsp Kosher Salt
2 tsp Black Pepper, coarse grind
3 TBSP Bacon fat

Sauce:

½ Cup Carrots, chopped
½ Cup Celery, chopped
1 Cup Yellow Onions, chopped
1 Cup Tomatillos, chopped
¼ Cup Garlic, minced
2 TBSP Chipotle Pepper in Adobo sauce, chopped
1 Bay Leaf
1 tsp Cumin
¾ tsp Oregano
¾ Cup White Wine, dry
1 ½ Cup Chicken Stock

1 TBSP Butter

Pre-heat the oven to 300 degrees.

Heat the Bacon fat over medium high heat in a sauce pot.

Season the Kurobuta Pork Shanks with Kosher Salt and Pepper, place in a single layer in the sauce pot and brown over medium to high heat on all sides, 8 – 10 minutes.

Remove from the sauce pot and place in one layer in a roasting pan.

Remove half of the fat from the sauce pot. Add the Carrots, Celery and Onions and sauté until the Onions are translucent, 5 – 8 minutes.

Add the Tomatillos, Garlic, Chipotle, Bay Leaf, Cumin, Oregano and sauté until the Garlic is fragrant, 3 – 5 minutes.
Add the White Wine, bring to a boil, then simmer until reduced by half.

Add the Chicken Stock to the sauce pot mixture and mix well.

Pour this mixture over the Pork Shanks in the roasting pan. Make sure that the Pork Shanks are evenly spaced in the pan.

Cover with parchment paper and then tightly with aluminum foil and place in the oven.

Set the timer for 2 hours. After 2 hours, turn the Shanks over in the pan, re-cover tightly and return to the oven for another 1 ½ hour. At the end of this time, check the Shanks for fork tenderness and return to the oven in 30 minute increments until they are fully cooked and tender.

196

Remove the Shanks from the roasting pan, place on a serving dish and cover loosely with foil to retain the heat.

Strain the braising liquid, placing the veggie solids in the bowl of a food processor and the liquid in a small sauce pot.

Remove the fat from the braising liquid. Bring the "fat free" liquid in the sauce pot to a boil then reduce the heat and simmer until it is reduced by half.

Place the strained veggie solids in the bowl of a food processor and puree.

Add about ¾ of the pureed veggies to the reduced liquid in the small sauce pot. Whisk in the butter slowly. Taste and adjust seasonings.

To serve, place a Pork Shank on a bed of Hand Mashed Potatoes (pg 157) and top with the Sauce.

Enjoy!

♣Beanery Moves

In our September, 2010 blog, I, Steph, recounted our move and wrote:

"Has it really been 26 years since the Brick Oven Bistro opened its doors? My, how time flies when you're having fun.

Those of you who have ever paused at the entrance to our restaurant have probably noticed some old black and white photos on the wall just as you walk in. One of those photos is of our original location at 5th and Main (the current home of Addie's). For those too young, or too recent, to recollect the story behind our relocation from there to our present site on The Grove at 8th and Main (what a difference three blocks can make!), it is a story worth re-telling.

It was only about five years after opening our doors that we realized we would need more space (we thank our customers for that necessity), and we began looking for a new location. As ideal as our current location may seem today, since we like to think of The Grove as the beating heart of downtown Boise, it was a very different sort of scene back in the late 80's. The Grove was quiet.

I remember as we were building our new restaurant, looking across the "plaza" that no one was walking by, or around...and the thought came to me, what were we thinking? There was no hotel and few events at the convention center in those days, so everyone from the banks walked out the door and toward other parts of

town. It was a bit daunting to say the least!

I remember years later talking to a friend from Argentina who arrived in Boise with her husband. She, like I, came from a country with plazas where people walked the plaza at night, where the plaza was the center of activity. She recalls waking up on a Sunday at the current Hotel 43 – then the Statehouse Inn - and looking down at the "plaza" where nothing was moving. She thought she had been brought to a wasteland!

But we believed in the potential of The Grove, and more importantly of our downtown Boise core; so with the passion and optimism of youth, we plunged boldly forward. To commemorate our move, we decided that we wanted an event more unique than a ribbon cutting. We decided on a "parade of chairs". Gathering up our employees and 30 of our customers, we congregated in the parking lot of the old restaurant and blew up balloons, tied them to the restaurant chairs and took off down Main Street. It was festive, fun and lighthearted -- attributes that we like to think characterize all that we do at the Brick Oven Bistro to this day.

I'm happy to say that our optimism has been vindicated by the test of time. We enjoy all the visitors that we get to engage with, and our location makes us feel as though we play the role of "Boise welcomers". The plaza has indeed become a plaza, with families and individuals enjoying the quiet and all the falling water. Children love the freedom of being able to wander to the water, feed the birds and ducks, while their parents appreciate a "fume-free", safe, and comfortable spot to be. We have helped enliven the plaza, bringing color, foliage and great food to the area – an added reason to walk around The Grove.

There is something about being in the center – for if you think of, it The Grove is indeed the center of downtown. It has been a delightful space – away from the bustle of autos and trucks – an oasis in the centre of a metropolis. And for us, it all started with a parade of chairs...and a leap of faith!"

Jeff and I thank the Oppenheimer's for trusting in us!

Jamaican Chicken Dinner

Our Jamaican Chicken Dinner with Bob Marley Sauce was inspired by an apple/almond stuffed chicken that we bought from our suppliers. Boned chicken thighs were wrapped around an apple/almond stuffing. In searching for an appropriate sauce to serve with it we decided that Jamaican jerk sauce would be just the ticket. While the Caribbean offers up a number of versions of jerk sauce, the common flavor denominator seems to be allspice. Rather than using chicken stock for the liquid, we use Marsala, which explains the nod to Jamaica's favorite son, the dreadlock king of reggae. We serve this dish with rice and greens, which would most likely be how you would enjoy it in Trenchtown, mon.

We have recreated this for you and trust us, it is better than the original!

8 Chicken Thighs or 4 Split Chickens

Jerk Rub:
1 Cup Green Onions, chopped
1 Habanero Pepper, seeded
3 Cloves Garlic
2 tsp Allspice
1 TBSP Thyme
2 tsp Kosher Salt
2 TBSP Dark Molasses
¼ Cup Canola Oil

Place all the ingredients in a food processor and puree fully.

Wash and dry the Chickens. Separate the skin from the meat with your hands and spread the rub between the skin and the meat.

Place on a platter, cover with plastic wrap and set in the refrigerator for at least 2 hours.

Half an hour before cooking, remove from the refrigerator and allow to come to room temperature prior to baking or grilling.

If Baking, preheat the oven to 375 degrees.

Place the rubbed Chickens on a baking sheet. Place in the oven or grill, until they reach the baking temperature you desire – 170 degrees was our target!

Bob Marley Sauce

½ Cup Marsala
2 ½ tsp Garlic, minced

¾ Cup Water
¾ tsp Chicken Base

1 ¾ Cups Corn Gravy Base (pg 166)
1 TBSP Honey
¼ tsp Allspice
½ tsp Nutmeg
Pinch Cayenne Pepper
Pinch White Pepper

Place the Marsala and Garlic into a sauté pan and over medium heat, reduce by half. Set aside for use later.

Mix the Water and Chicken Base fully. Set aside for use later

Place the Corn Gravy Base, Honey, Allspice, Nutmeg, Cayenne and White Pepper in a sauce pot.

Strain the Marsala reduction into the sauce pot.

Add ½ Cup of the Chicken stock to the sauce pot and whisk until smooth. Over medium high heat bring to a simmer. Simmer for 10 minutes.
Add the remaining Chicken stock, stirring constantly until Nirvana or a smooth consistency is reached, whichever comes first.
*if neither, consider a new avocation. (original instructions!)

♣I'd Love to!

One day after yet another "Thank you" expressed to a person was met with "No problem", we knew it was time to address communication with our staff.

They were used to language lessons. We were and are English teachers. So, when greeted and asked "How are you?" and they responded "Not bad", they learned about double negatives and were asked, "Are you ok, wonderful, good?"

It was and is difficult, when a "Thank you" elicits a "No problem", to wonder what the exact problem might be with the "Thank you". How much better does it feel when you hear a "You're welcome" or better yet, "My pleasure!"

There were many questions we and our staff were asked in a day to which the answer might perhaps have to be "No." It never felt good to us to say "No". The word "No" does not fit with the concept of hospitality that we believe. That was when "I'd love to", occurred to us.

What if any question was first met with an "I'd love to" and followed, if needed, with an explanation of why that could not happen. We shared this notion of communication with our managers and staff and we all tried it out. At the end of the day, the guests felt better, and we felt better! We were able to really fulfill the definition of hospitality, greeting guests and strangers with genuine warmth and kindness.

BBQ Mexican Chicken

It was only in recent years that a variety of Mexican Pepper Powders came onto Boise's markets, and when they did, we took advantage of the richness of flavors that they added to standard recipes. This BBQ Chicken is a delicious example of the creativity they inspired. We baked these in the restaurant and the recipe is written for baking. They are great grilled as well!

8 Chicken Thighs or 4 Split Chickens

Dry Rub:
1 TBSP Ancho Pepper Powder
1 TBSP Chipotle Pepper Powder
1 tsp Cumin
1 tsp Onion Powder
1 tsp Kosher Salt
1 tsp Black Pepper, coarse grind

BBQ Sauce:
¾ Cup Honey
2 ea Chipotle Peppers in Adobo Sauce
1 TBSP Adobo Sauce
2 TBSP Lime Juice

Wash and dry the Chickens.

Place all the ingredients for the dry rub in a small bowl, mix well.

Rub the Dry Rub into all sides of the Chickens. Place on a platter, cover with plastic wrap and set in the refrigerator for at least 2 hours. Half an hour before cooking, remove from the refrigerator and allow to come to room temperature prior to baking.

Preheat the oven to 375 degrees.

Place the rubbed Chickens on a baking sheet and brush with the BBQ Sauce. Bake in the oven, until they reach the baking temperature you desire – 170 degrees was our target!

Sunday Country Pork Roast

In our blog in 2010, we wrote: "Move over free-range chicken and Kobe beef and make way for "the other white meat." You may have noticed that for awhile now, the Brick Oven Bistro has been featuring Kurobuta pork on its menu, courtesy of local provider Snake River Farms. Kurobuta (Japanese for "black hog") has a nearly 300 year history, going back to the discovery of Berkshire hogs by the army of Oliver Cromwell.

While things didn't turn out all that well for Ollie and his gang, Berkshire hogs set the industry standard for pork for their consistently exquisite taste. When the British gave a gift of the hogs to a Japanese diplomat, the meat that was to become

Kurobuta Pork soon took its place beside Kobe beef as a celebrated cuisine icon.

So, how good is Kurobuta Pork? How's this? Awhile back, the National Pork Producers Council conducted a taste test based on 25 quality traits --and Kurobuta Pork ranked #1 of 19 of them, including tenderness and juiciness. You can experience this same treat every Sunday on the Brick Oven Bistro menu, where we are especially proud to be offering this delicacy. Come and experience Kurobuta pork for yourself, and see what all the fuss is about."

Locally, for those of you interested in purchasing Snake River Farms Kurobuta Pork, do go to Meats Royale on Overland Rd.!

Generally the pieces of Kurobuta Pork loin that we served were 3 – 4 pounds. We always brined them for 3 hours prior to roasting them.

Brine for a 4 pound loin:
1 Qt Water
⅓ Cup Cider Vinegar
2 ½ TBSP Table Salt
1 ½ TBSP Brown Sugar
4 tsp Juniper Berries

Seasoning for Pork Loin:
2 tsp Olive Oil
1 tsp Black Pepper, coarse grind
1 tsp Kosher Salt
2 tsp Rosemary

Mix all the Brine ingredients together. Make sure to dissolve fully the Brown Sugar and Table Salt. Place the Pork in the Brine. Cover and place in the refrigerator for 3 hours.

After 3 hours, remove from the brine and fully dry.

Pre-heat the oven to 325 degrees.

206

Preheat a cast iron pan or griddle over high heat.

Brush the Pork Loin with the Olive Oil and then sprinkle all over with the spices, rubbing these into the meat

Place the roast in the pan and sear all sides.

Remove from the pan or griddle and place on a baking sheet pan in the oven.

Roast until the internal temperature is 140 degrees. It will take about an hour.

Remove from the oven, covering the roast lightly with foil, and let them rest for a twenty minutes before slicing.

Yield is about 3 dinner servings per pound of Pork.

We served our dinner with Hand-Mashed Potatoes, Creamy Country Corn Gravy, Blushing Applesauce, Baby Carrots, a Garden Salad & freshly baked Bread!

Roast Garlic Pork with a Raspberry Chipotle Sauce

Snake River Farms Kurobuta Pork Loins and spice inspired this
variation. The Glaze would be great as well on a Flank Steak or a
Country Ham.

Pork:
8 Cloves Garlic
1 TBSP Rosemary, fresh
1 TBSP Sage, fresh
1 TBSP Thyme, fresh
1 tsp Kosher Salt
1 tsp Black pepper, coarse grind
3 TBSP Olive Oil

1 Pork Loin

Sauce:
4 Cups Frozen Raspberries
1 ¾ Cups Water
1 ½ tsp Chicken Base

½ of a 7 oz Can of Chipotles in Adobo Sauce, pureed

2 TBSP Cider Vinegar
2 TBSP Honey
1 tsp Smoked Hot Paprika
1 tsp Kosher Salt

1 TBSP Corn Starch

¼ Cup Water

4 TBSP Butter, cut into 4 pieces

Pork:

Place the Garlic, Rosemary, Sage, Thyme, Salt and Pepper in a food processor and pulse to chop. Add the oil slowly to make a spreadable paste.

Preheat the oven to 325 degrees.

Over the burners, pre-heat a cast iron pan or griddle.

Season the Pork Loin with Salt and Pepper. Sear the Pork Loin on all sides. Remove from the heat.

Rub the Garlic/herb mixture over the Pork Loin.

Place in a baking dish and roast to 140 degrees. Five minutes before removing from the oven evenly spread some of the Raspberry Chipotle Sauce over the Pork.

Remove from the oven, covering the roast lightly with foil, and let them rest for twenty minutes before slicing.

Yield is about 3 dinner servings per pound of Pork.

Sauce:

Place the Raspberries, Water and Chicken Base in a sauce pot.

Add the pureed Chipotles, Cider Vinegar, Honey, Smoked Hot Paprika and Salt into the sauce pot and bring to a boil. Turn the heat off.

Puree the contents using a blender.
With a fine strainer, strain the pureed sauce into a large sauté pan.

Mix the Corn Starch and the Water to form a slurry.

Pour the Corn Starch slurry into the pureed Sauce in the sauté pan, and heat over medium high heat until the Sauce thickens.

Whisk the Butter into the sauce, one piece at a time. Reduce the heat to low until ready to serve.

Crawfish Etouffee

In our blog, October 2009, we wrote, "Our crawfish etouffee is NOT an acquired taste. As we used to say about the Grateful Dead, "you're either on the bus or you're off the bus." When it comes to crawfish etouffee, if you don't "get it" with the first spoonful, you sure as heck won't get it with the second...or third.

It's because of our deep respect for you, those of you on the crawfish etouffee bus, that we write this blog. We have something important to tell you -- but first you need to get yourself a glass of wine, sit down, and take a deep breath.

We've altered the crawfish etouffee recipe. We'll now give you a few moments to fully absorb the impact of this statement. Have you finished hyperventilating? If so, let us explain.

Ever since we added crawfish etouffee to the Brick Oven Bistro menu, we've been making it with a lobster base. It was the very best lobster base we could find, but let's face it, when it come to access to lobster, we're at a bit of a disadvantage here in the City of Trees. It appears, for starters, that we've pretty much fished out the native lobster population from the Boise River. But not long ago we found a source for something that will forever change our crawfish etouffee: lobster bodies.

I know it sounds a bit ghoulish, but when sitting down to a celebratory meal of lobster tails, haven't you ever been the least bit curious about what happened to the rest of the crustacean? The answer is that some enterprising producers have been quick freezing the bodies and sending them to the Brick Oven Bistro (alright, I'm sure others are buying them as well, but they can write their own blogs). In place of lobster base, we are now using lobster bodies to make the stock for our crawfish etouffee.

Why are we doing this? For starters, we just don't believe that "great" is good enough if you can up the culinary ante. Making our soup base with lobster bodies gives our crawfish etouffee a much greater intensity and richness. Besides, we have continually lusted after the taste of etouffee that we cultivated at our favorite source in Houston, Texas (we'll be happy to divulge the name if you're interested). We're not quite there...but we're getting close. For now, we're going to leave judgement of our efforts to you...you etouffee elite, you crawfish cognoscenti, you cravers of Cajun!"

Lobster Stock

This recipe yields 1 ½ Gallons, more than you will need for a batch of Etouffee. You can certainly reduce the recipe, however we always like having some on hand, so we freeze what we do not use!

2 TBSP Olive Oil
1 ½ Cups Carrots, coin cut
1 ½ Cups Celery, chopped
6 Cups Yellow Onions, chopped
10 Garlic cloves, chopped
2 Bay Leaves
1 Cup Parsley Stems
1 ½ tsp Thyme
1 12 oz Can Tomato Paste

2 Cups dry White Wine

2 ½ Gallons Water
1 ¼ Lb Lobster Bodies

In a large stock pot, heat the oil and sweat the Carrots, Celery, Yellow Onions, Garlic, Bay leaves, Parsley, Thyme and Tomato Paste until soft.

Add the White Wine and reduce until there is almost none left.

Add the Water and the Lobster Bodies, bring to a boil and then reduce to a simmer.

Simmer until you have about 1 ½ Gallons remaining.

Throughout the cooking process, periodically skim the surface to remove impurities.

When ready, strain through a colander lined with cheesecloth. Press down to remove every drop of liquid that is in the mixture.

Bistro Crawfish Etouffee

And with the stock made, here comes "the rest of the story"! For the roux, in order to consistently reach the right color, we found a paint chip, Behr Olympic Bronze UL 150-17 which we laminated and gave to our cooks to use as their color goal!

Roux:
⅜ Lb Butter (1 ½ sticks or 12 TBSP)
1 ¼ Cup Flour, all purpose

Etouffee:
⅓ Lb Shrimp raw, peeled and devined
⅔ Cup Water

1 TBSP Canola Oil
1 tsp Anchovy Paste
½ tsp Cayenne Pepper

2 ¼ Cup Celery, sliced
2 ¼ Cup Yellow Onion, diced

2 ¼ Cup Green Pepper diced

1 ½ Qts Mushrooms sliced
3 TBSP Garlic, minced

1 TBSP Butter

2 TBSP Brandy
3 TBSP Paprika
¼ tsp Black Pepper
¼ tsp White Pepper
1 TBSP Kosher Salt

2 Qts Lobster Stock
1 ½ Lbs Crawfish tails

1 Cup Whole Milk
1 Cup Heavy Cream

Roux preparation: In a sauté pan over medium heat, melt the Butter then add the Flour whisking constantly. Continue cooking and whisking until it is the color of brown sugar. We encourage you to use the paint chip mentioned above. Set aside to cool, for later use.

Place the Shrimp and water in a food processor and puree until smooth. Set aside for later use.

Heat the Canola Oil over medium heat in a large sauce pot. Add the Anchovy Paste and Cayenne and dissolve this into the oil.

Add the Celery, Onion and Green Pepper and sauté until the Onions are translucent.

Add the Garlic and Mushroom and continue to sauté for 4 minutes.

Add the Butter to the sauce pot to melt.

Add the Spices and Brandy to the sauce pot and continue to sauté for 3 more minutes.

Add the Lobster stock to the sauce pot.

Add the Crawfish with their juices and the pureed Shrimp. Bring all ingredients to a boil.

Gradually whisk in the Roux. When fully incorporated, reduce the heat and simmer for 10 minutes.

Whisk the Milk and Heavy Cream into the sauce pot and bring back to temperature.

Taste and adjust seasonings.

This meal is served in a large shallow soup bowl with a scoop of Veggie Rice (Pg 160) on the bottom, then the Etouffee, topped with chopped Green Onions.

Yield is 1 Gallon.

Shrimp Gazpacho

Savor Idaho, the Idaho Wine Commission June event at the Idaho Botanical Garden is a great event which we participated in annually. This was our well-received contribution to the event. Refreshing on a hot day, equally as delicious heated up!

For the Shrimp stock called for in this recipe, we used a high quality shrimp base which we sourced from Schreiber Foods. It is difficult to find in local markets, so we have included our Shrimp Stock recipe. We trust you purchase frozen shell-on shrimp, when you choose to eat shrimp. We encourage you to do so. When using these, remove the shells, prior to preparing the shrimp meat, and freeze the shells for use in this stock.

Shrimp Stock

1 ½ Lbs Shrimp shells, thawed and roasted

1 ½ Qts Water
1 ½ tsp Garlic, chopped
½ Cup Yellow Onions, chopped
¼ Cup Carrots, chopped
¼ Cup Celery, chopped
¼ Cup Mushrooms, chopped

Bouquet Garni:
1 Bay Leaf
¼ tsp Thyme
⅛ tsp Black Peppercorns
2 Parsley stems, chopped

Preheat the oven to 300 degrees.

Place the Shrimp shells on a baking tray and bake for 15-20 minutes, until the shells are lightly toasted.

Place the toasted Shrimp shells in a large sauce pot with the water and veggies.

Wrap the Bouquet Garni in a piece of cheese cloth or in a coffee filter, tie with a piece of string and place in the sauce pot with the rest of the ingredients.

Bring to a boil and then lower to a simmer. Simmer for 1 ½ hours, periodically skimming the impurities from the surface.

Taste. If you wish a stronger flavor, bring to a boil. Boil vigorously until the desired flavor is reached.

Yield is 1 Quart.

If you have more stock than you need, freeze it for use later. Frozen stock is a cook's bounty!

Shrimp Gazpacho

With the stock on hand, here is the "rest of the story". We have made this recipe both with Salad Shrimp and with 72/90 frozen shrimp. We prefer using the larger 72/90's which we cook and then cut in half. It is good both ways.

3 Lbs Shrimp, raw, peeled and devined

¼ Cup Canola Oil

¼ Cup Garlic, chopped
1 Cup Celery, chopped
1 Cup Green Peppers, chopped
1 Cup Yellow Onions, chopped

¼ Cup All Purpose Flour

1 tsp Basil
1 tsp Marjoram
¾ tsp Oregano
¾ tsp Thyme
¾ tsp Black Pepper, coarse grind
¼ tsp White Pepper
¼ tsp Kosher Salt
1 ½ tsp Brown Sugar
¾ tsp Tabasco

2 ½ Cups Water
2 TBSP Shrimp Base
or
2 ½ Cups Shrimp Stock

5 Cups Crushed Tomatoes

¼ Cup Parsley, flat leaf chopped
½ Cup Green Onions, chopped

If you are using the 72/90 shrimp, cook them in the Shrimp Stock, remove and cool them. Once cool, cut them in half, and set them aside to add in at the end of the preparation. Generally Salad Shrimp comes cooked, so it is simply added to the Gazpacho at the end of the preparation as noted in this recipe.

Heat the Canola Oil in a large sauce pot. Add the Garlic, Celery, Peppers and Onions and sauté over medium high heat until softened but not browned.

Add the flour, mix thoroughly and allow this to cook for about 4 minutes over medium heat.

Add the spices and Shrimp stock and mix.

Add the canned Tomatoes, Parsley and Green Onions and simmer for 15 minutes.

Add the shrimp and simmer for an additional 5 minutes.

Place in the refrigerator to cool. Serve topped with Chives.

Bistro Quiche

We have enjoyed many different varieties of Quiche. Ours is creamy and flavorful, best served warm! If you enjoy making your own crust, do look at the Vodka Pie Crust recipe from America's Test Kitchen. It is amazingly simple and turns out perfectly each time. At the restaurant, we usually used a pre-made frozen crust, one of our few attempts to simplify production! We made both a Quiche Lorraine and a Veggie Quiche, and have included the fillings below. We used a variety of cheeses. Our last blend was Provolone Mozzarella. At home we usually use a Gruyere.

Pie Crust, frozen

Filling for 1 Quiche Lorraine:
¾ Cup Yellow Onions, diced
½ Cup Green Pepper, diced
½ Cup Bacon, cooked and diced

Filling for 1 Veggie Quiche:
¾ Cup Yellow Onion, diced
½ Cup Green Pepper, diced
½ Cup Mushrooms, diced

For 1 Quiche:
2 ¼ tsp Cornstarch
¾ Cup Milk
¾ Cup Heavy Cream

4 Eggs
1 Egg Yolk
¼ tsp Kosher Salt
⅛ tsp Black Pepper, coarse grind
Pinch Cayenne Pepper
Pinch Nutmeg

1 TBSP Parsley

½ Cup Cheese, grated

Preheat the oven to 325 degrees.

Place the frozen crust on a sheet pan, weight it down with pie weights and bake for 10 minutes.

Remove from the oven, remove the pie weights and cool.

Increase the heat in the oven to 350 degrees.

Place the Vegetables (and Bacon if making a Lorraine) in a sauce pan and sauté until tender. Set aside to cool.

Place the Cornstarch, Milk, Heavy Cream, Eggs, Egg Yolk and spices in a large bowl and whisk fully.

Place the reserved cooled Vegetables in the bottom of the Crust.

Top them with ¼ Cup of the Cheese. Sprinkle with the Parsley

Add the Milk/Egg mixture and Top with the remaining Cheese.

Bake for approximately 30 minutes until the center is set.

♣Getting close to your meal or the benefits of standing in line.

Bistro Blog August 3, 2009

The term "comfort food" conjures up similar emotions in most of us: a feeling of well being that we associate not simply with what we eat, but the context in which it is eaten.

We remember the sense that all was right with the world when we walked into our family kitchen on a chilly winter day to the welcoming fragrance of Mom's special meat loaf, Granny's Old World spaghetti Bolognese, Aunt Helen's fried chicken…or maybe the lamb biryani that was a favorite of Uncle Ramachandra.

221

The point is, "comfort food" is much more than a few hackneyed Mac and cheese stereotypes. It's food that was usually slow cooked, ladled into bowls or plates by someone we loved, and served up in a place that insulated us from a crazy and impersonal world outside the familiar walls we called home.

If we were to try and capture the culinary mission of the Brick Oven Bistro in just a few words, I think we'd describe it as "the constant effort to fill the comfort food void in the hearts and tummies of our customers." For some, this might be our meat loaf, our Yankee pot roast, or one of our soups or stews. For others, however, it might be something that they've never even

tasted before…like our new garlic roasted Kurobuta pork loin with raspberry chipotle candied glaze.

There's another aspect of comfort food that I don't think receives its due: the anticipation that comes from watching a meal being prepared. Over the years, we've found this to be an unexpected benefit to having our guests line up for their food. What started as a matter of convenience has become a unique experience that is a Brick Oven trademark.

Next time you join us for a meal, watch the interactions that take place in the serving line. People talk to our staff and to each other about the food that is being prepared right in front of them. Maybe they ask questions about how it was cooked, or what's in it. Or perhaps they compare their experiences with different menu items, share their personal favorites and the reasons they find it so hard to order something other than their comfort food of choice.

The net effect of all this, we hope, is that our guests come away with a feeling that one of them recently described as being "like a hug from the inside out." Now that I think of it, maybe that's the very best description of comfort food…and of the Brick Oven Bistro's culinary mission. Next time you need a hug, you know where to find us.

Bacon Spinach Strata or Spinach Strata

Some Saturdays we would serve Strata rather than our Quiche. Both are delicious. This recipe is wonderful as it is best when made the evening ahead of time, allowed to sit refrigerated overnight and baked in the morning! To make the Spinach Strata, remove the Bacon from the recipe. We generally used Provolone Mozzarella Cheese, however it is equally good with other cheese choices.

> 3 Loaves French bread sliced 1/2" wide.
> 5 TBSP Butter
>
> ¾ Cup White Wine
>
> 3 TBSP Butter
> ¾ Cup Yellow Onions, diced
>
> 1 Lb Frozen Spinach, thawed and well drained
>
> ⅓ Cup Bacon, cooked and chopped
>
> 9 Eggs, large
> 1 ½ Cups Heavy Cream
> 1 Cup + 2 TBSP Milk
> 1 ½ tsp Kosher Salt
> 1 ½ tsp Black Pepper, coarse grind
>
> 1 ½ Cups Cheese, grated

Slice the Bread, Butter on one side and set aside for use later.

Place the White Wine in a sauce pan and reduce by half. Set aside.

Place the Butter and Onions in a sauce pan and sauté until soft.

Add the Spinach and Bacon and sauté. Set aside for use later.

Place the Eggs in a large bowl and whisk until frothy.

Add the Heavy Cream, Milk and spices to the Eggs and whisk.

Add the cooled Wine reduction to the bowl and whisk.

Butter a 9" x 12" baking dish and arrange half of the buttered bread sliced, butter side up covering fully the bottom of the pan.

Spread half of the cooled Vegetable and Bacon mixture on top.

Spread ¾ Cup of the Cheese evenly on top.

Repeat the steps making a second layer.

Pour the Egg mixture on top and down the sides evenly.

Cover the surface with plastic wrap, place in the refrigerator and lightly weight it down.

The next morning, preheat the oven to 300 degrees. Remove the Strata pan from the refrigerator and allow it to come to room temperature (about 20 minutes). Remove the plastic wrap, place in the oven and bake for approximately 45 minutes.

Remove from the oven and let it sit for 20 minutes before serving. Top with a dollop of sour cream.

 # Eat Dessert First!

Life is short. Eat Dessert First!

The fact is that we took dessert every bit as seriously as any of our menu entrees. Desserts were a long-standing part of the Brick Oven Bistro tradition. Once in talking to a guest, I learned that he first visited us more than 15 years earlier because he had heard that we made the best milkshakes in town – then discovered to his surprise that we were actually a restaurant and not a soda fountain.

Our dessert tradition began whimsically enough with unique milkshake creations such as the Fuzzy Navel, New York Cheesecake, Bananas Foster, and Mom's Apple Pie – all of which continued to be made the old-fashioned way with high quality hard ice cream. Our friend and Denver food diva Pat Miller contributed her infamous Triple Fudge Nut Brownie, and we began baking Chocolate Chip and Almond Sugar cookies. As time went by, we further expanded our dessert portfolio with favorites such as our Apple Bread Pudding with Bourbon Walnut Sauce and our summer dessert standard, Strawberry Shortcake.

Not content to rest on our laurels, we continued to experiment with new dessert items —our Chocolate Espresso Pecan Pie and our Reese's Peanut Butter Cup Chocolate Chip Cheesecake, which proved that when it comes to dessert, less is definitely not more.

While most of our guests didn't have a whole lot of room left over when they finished up a Brick Oven Bistro lunch or dinner entrée, there were plenty who enjoyed sharing a dessert or took one home to eat later.

We were proud of our dessert tradition and delighted that so many folks made our cookies and brownies a highlight of their working day. Sure, you could call that indulgence, but we preferred to think of it as simply getting your "just desserts" in life.

Pat's Triple Fudge Nut Brownies

This is a most amazing recipe, the likes of which we have not often seen in any cookbook. There are some critical points to follow. The temperature of the melted Butter and Chocolate must be close to 110 degrees. Too hot or too cold and these Brownies do not turn out. There is some nuance when baking these as well, as you must watch the Marshmallows carefully. They will be just on the brink of cracking when the recipe is perfectly baked. Teaching this recipe was always rewarding as when the cook got these right, they felt great and had added many miles to their baking patience!

½ Lb Butter
1 Cup Dream Semi-sweet Chocolate Chips
¾ Lb Dream Bittersweet Chocolate wafers

4 Eggs at room temperature

2 TBSP Vanilla

1 ¾ Cups Granulated Sugar
¼ Cup Brown Sugar
1 TBSP Cocoa Powder, high quality - it matters!

1 Cup White Flour

1 Cup Walnuts, ¼ inch chop
2 Cups Marshmallows, mini

Preheat standard oven to 315 degrees, convection oven to 300 degrees.

Prepare a 9"x 12" baking pan by greasing the bottom and sides with softened butter and then placing a piece of parchment paper on the bottom and greasing it with softened butter.

Cut the Butter into small pieces and place the Butter, Chocolate Chips and Bittersweet Chocolate in a double boiler. Let the ingredients melt together, whisking as needed to blend. When melted, set aside to cool to 110 degrees.

Place all the eggs into a mixing bowl with a wire whip attachment and beat until the eggs are white and frothy.

Add the Vanilla and beat until blended.

Change to the paddle attachment on the mixer and add the Sugars and Cocoa to the bowl. Mix until fully blended.

Add the cooled Butter and Chocolate mixture and beat until smooth

Add the Flour to the mixing bowl and beat until barely blended.

Remove the bowl from the mixer and mix the Walnuts and Marshmallows by hand until evenly blended into the mixture.

Pour into the prepared pan and bake immediately for approximately 30 minutes.

As mentioned in the introduction above, the Marshmallows will be puffed but not cracking, and a toothpick will come out clean.

Allow to cool, preferably overnight. Once at room temperature, you can store these, covered with plastic wrap in a refrigerator and cut them once fully cool.

Yield is 10 pieces.

Golden Carrot Cake with Cream Cheese Frosting

My goodness, the number of times we baked, in search of a Carrot Cake that had great flavor and would remain moist longer than a day! This batter will appear to be much more moist than most, intentionally. It works. We even know some local musicians who refused to play on our patio until they had their obligatory Brick Oven Bistro Carrot Cake. Blessings be on you, Kevin Kirk!

½ Lb. Butter, at room temperature

2 Cups Granulated Sugar

2 Eggs, at room temperature

½ Cup All Purpose Flour
½ Cup Bread Flour
¾ Cup Wheat Flour
½ Cup +2 TBSP Wheat Bran

1 tsp Allspice
1 ½ tsp Cinnamon
1 tsp Cloves
1 tsp Nutmeg
1 TBSP Baking Powder
½ tsp Table Salt

½ Cup Hot Water

¾ Cup Carrots, peeled and finely grated
1 Cup Walnuts, chopped
 Crushed Pineapple, drained of all juice

Pre-heat a standard oven to 315 degrees, a convection oven to 300 degrees.

Prepare your baking pan by greasing with butter and then flouring a 6" x 8 ½" cake pan.

Place the Butter in a mixer bowl and cream until smooth.

Slowly add the Sugar mixing it in completely.

Add the Eggs, one at a time until fully mixed.

In a separate bowl, whisk the flours with all of the spices.

Add half the flour mixture and half the hot water at a time and mix.

Remove from the mixer and add the remaining Carrots, Walnuts and Pineapple, folding them in by hand.

Smooth the batter and then bake for 30 -40 minutes, checking with a toothpick to insure that the middle is done. The toothpick will come out clean.

If the top is getting too brown, cover loosely with foil.

Cool in the pan. Yield is 8 – 10 pieces, depending on your cut!

Cream Cheese Frosting for Golden Carrot Cake

This is a simple and versatile frosting that works well on many different cakes.

232

> 1 Lb Cream Cheese, at room temperature
> 6 TBSP Butter, at room temperature
>
> 2 ¼ tsp Vanilla Extract
>
> 7 ½ Cups Confectioners Sugar

Place the Cream Cheese and the Butter in a mixer and cream until completely mixed together.

Add the remaining ingredients and mix until smooth and spreadable.

♣ The Bistro "We"

To make our restaurant hum, we had to work together. Every person helped in the kitchen, helped in the dining room and helped with clean up. This included the managers, Jeff and I. In many restaurants there is a hierarchy, which we found to be counterproductive. From the beginning we did not hire people to just be dishwashers. Everyone in the restaurant washed dishes and learned how to do the positions on the service line or on the cooking line. If someone was unable to come to work, we could turn to another staff member to fill the position. As we shared always, "There is no I in team!"

Chocolate Chip Cookies

This recipe was the final result of way too many experiments! We wanted a large cookie that was not too heavy, but one that would not fall apart. There are some interesting ideas we found on our way to this recipe. One was to create a ¼ inch hole in the middle of the cookie so that the center would fill in and be cooked at the same time as the edges. This we found was not the answer. For us, the answer was in making the cookies ahead of time, pressing them into individual cookies, cooling them and then cooking them from cool when we needed them. In this way, we always had cookies to add and they baked beautifully. With pressed cookies, ready to go in the refrigerator, freshly baked cookies are easy and wonderful!

½ Lb Butter, room temperature
1 ½ Cups Brown Sugar, packed
½ Cup White Sugar

3 Egg Yolks, room temperature
2 Eggs, room temperature
4 tsp Vanilla

1 ¾ Cups Bread Flour
2 Cups All Purpose Flour
1 ½ tsp Table Salt
1 ½ tsp Baking Soda

2 Cups Chocolate Chips

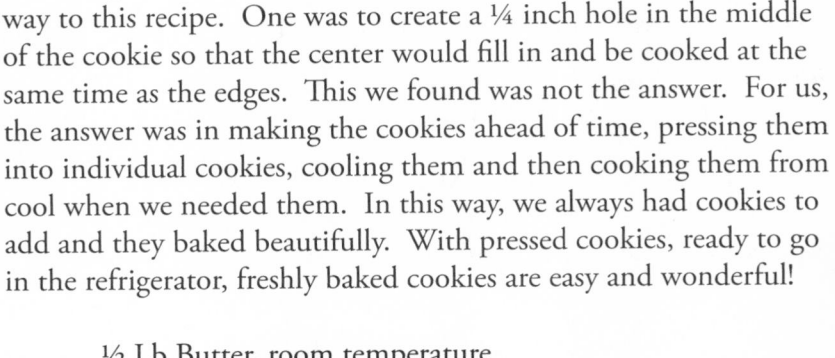

Blend Butter and Sugars in Mixer bowl and mix until smooth

Whisk the Egg Yolks, Eggs and Vanilla into a bowl and add to the Butter and Sugars and mix until smooth.

Whisk the Flours, Salt and Baking Soda in a bowl. Add to the Mixer bowl and mix until most of the Flour mixture is incorporated. Do not over mix as the cookies will get hard!

234

Add the Chocolate Chips and mix in quickly, about 20 seconds. If you need to do any final mixing, do it by hand.

Portion the mix into 20 cookies, press them individually into a 3 inch circle, separate them using patty papers and let them cool for at least 6 hours before baking.

Preheat standard oven to 325 degrees, convection oven to 300 degrees. Place the cookies on a parchment lined cookie sheet and bake for 9-11 minutes until done.   Yield is 20 Cookies.

Almond Sugar Cookies

This cookie's aficionados are legendary in their affection for this sugary delight. As with our Chocolate Chip Cookies, these are best when made ahead of time and baked from cold.

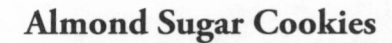

¾ Lb Butter, room temperature
2 ½ Cups White Sugar

2 Eggs, room temperature

½ tsp Almond Extract

5 Cups Flour
¼ tsp Baking Powder
½ tsp Table Salt

¼ Cup Milk

Blend Butter and Sugar in Mixer bowl and mix until smooth

Add the Eggs one at a time to the Butter and Sugar and mix until completely blended and smooth, before adding the second one. Add the Almond Extract and mix until blended.

Whisk the Flours, Baking Powder and Salt in a bowl.

Add half of the Flour mixture and half of the Milk at a time, then follow with the second half of these. Mix until fully blended, but do not over mix as the cookies will get hard!

235

Portion the mix into 20 cookies, press them individually into a 3 inch circle, separate them using patty papers and let them cool for at least 6 hours before baking.

Preheat standard oven to 325 degrees, convection oven to 300 degrees.

Place the cookies on a parchment lined cookie sheet and bake for 9-11 minutes until lightly browned on the edges. Cool and then frost.

Yield is 15 Cookies.

Almond Sugar Cookie Frosting

Simple to make, this is the perfect topping for the cookies. This is a great spice cupcake or cake frosting as well. The recipe can be doubled or tripled as needed. If you have any left over after frosting the cookies, or if you are baking the cookies at different times, store the remaining frosting in the refrigerator. The cookies are easiest to frost Be sure to let the amount you need get to room temperature before frosting cookies.

¼ Lb Butter, at room temperature

2 ¼ Cups Confectioners Sugar
¼ tsp Salt

3 TBSP Milk
⅛ tsp Almond Extract

Place the Butter in a mixer bowl and mix until creamy.

Add the remaining ingredients and mix until smooth. Add more milk if needed.

Apple Bread Pudding with Bourbon Walnut Sauce

We'd like to share a little something about this Brick Oven Bistro dessert classic: our bread pudding. True story: a number of years ago, I overheard a conversation between two customers in our serving line. One of them had noticed that bread pudding was on our list of desserts. "Man, I love bread pudding," he opined. The other nodded and said, "So do I, but the best bread pudding I've ever had came from a restaurant in New Orleans." I couldn't help jumping in. "That wouldn't have been Brennan's, would it?" I asked. "As a matter of fact, it was," he said, with some surprise.

We love Brennan's bread pudding as well, which is why we "reverse engineered" their recipe with some little tweaks of our own to offer up just a bit of that Crescent City flavor to our own City of Trees. The point to all this is that when you love good food, you can't help but want to share the best of what you experience in your travels.

New Orleans is a legendary place to eat, with a lot of recipes worth emulating (and we emulated a few for our menu), but great food is everywhere...so we just kept on doing our homework and sharing the best of what we found. It was tough job, but someone had to do it! Now, pass me the Bourbon Walnut sauce!

> 2- 12" Loaves French Bread cut into 1 inch cubes
> 2- 12" Loaves Wheat Bread cut into 1 inch cubes (total weight of bread is 1 ¼ Lbs)

7 TBSP Butter, melted and slightly cooled

5 Eggs, large
4 Egg Yolks

2 ½ tsp Vanilla
1 ¼ Cup Granulated Sugar
4 tsp Cinnamon

2 ½ Cups Whole Milk
2 ¾ Cups Heavy Cream

¾ Cup Apple Cobbler Filling

Place the eggs and egg yolks in a mixer and whisk until frothy.

Into the melted butter, mix a tablespoon of the egg mixture, then place all of the melted butter and egg into the mixer bowl and whisk until blended
Add the Vanilla, Granulated Sugar and Cinnamon to the mixer bowl and whisk until blended.

Add the Milk and the Heavy Cream and whisk until blended.

Add the Apple Pie Filling and whisk until blended.

Place the bread cubes into a 9 x 12 inch baking pan. Add the Egg and Milk mixture and gently fold this in.

Cover the baking pan with aluminum foil and place in the refrigerator for at least one hour, if not overnight. When ready to bake, let the pan sit out for 20 minutes.

Place in a pre-heated 350 degree oven for 40 minutes, with the aluminum foil cover on, then remove the cover and bake for an additional 10 – 15 minutes, until the custard is set and the top is browned.

To serve: Cut into nine 3"x 4" servings, top with Bourbon Walnut Sauce and freshly whipped Cream.

Bourbon Walnut Sauce

¼ Lb Butter

1 Cup Granulated Sugar

1 Oz Bourbon

1 Egg, beaten

3 TBSP Walnuts, chopped

Melt the butter over medium heat in a medium sized saucepan.

Add the Sugar to the melted butter and whisk to completely incorporate and until the mixture begins to bubble. This will be about 5 minutes of constant whisking.

Take the saucepan off the heat and very carefully and slowly, mix in the Bourbon. It will foam up, so be careful.

Immediately whisk in the beaten Egg and chopped Walnuts, until completely blended. Serve!

Fresh Strawberry Shortcake

As Strawberries came into season, we would serve this most loved dessert. In the weeks leading up to the season, guests would come in asking for the "launch date". We always made our biscuits so that this dessert could be shared, often however the order would come back for the second one or third one, as family members longed for tastes and were asked to "get your own!". Fresh Strawberries long for Freshly Whipped Cream, please go the extra step to do this, and do make your own shortcakes!

We made many different shortcake recipes over the years. Our favorite, the simplest and the one we recommend is James Beard's Cream Biscuit recipe. We encourage you to use it. You can find it in his wonderful book, <u>Beard on Bread</u>.

> 2 Qts Strawberries, rinsed, hulled and sliced
>
> 2 ½ TBSP Granulated Sugar
> ½ tsp Triple Sec

Place the sliced Strawberries in a bowl. Sprinkle them with the Sugar and the Triple Sec. Mix gently. Place in the refrigerator for at least 2 hours, so that the flavors meld.

Food should be prepared with Butter and Love
Swedish Proverb

Freshly Whipped Cream

When making our Whipped Cream, we used a Vanilla Syrup to sweeten the Cream. Add this after you have whipped the Cream. It is so easy to whip this by hand, just be sure to have all the ingredients and the whisk and bowl cold!

> 2 Cups Heavy Cream
> ½ tsp Vanilla Syrup

Whip by hand with a large bulb whisk or use a mixer!

The order is Half a Biscuit, Whipped Cream, Strawberries, Half a Biscuit, Strawberries, Whipped Cream!

♣ *Shared Memories*

The Beanery has always been a favorite, but it became a family tradition.
When I finally safely delivered my first child, I had not eaten for 20 hours. Just ice chips. I was starving and my timing was bad. The kitchen and the cafeteria were closed. The only "food" available was jello. My wonderful husband said "I'll be back" and when he returned he had my favorite sandwich and side from the Beanery. I almost cried, it was so good.
It became a tradition after everyone of our children were born.
Thank you for all the wonderful years filled with great food, conscientious service and indelible memories.   Helen M.

Chocolate Espresso Pecan Pie

"I can't think of anyone who would not love these tastes and textures!" The chef and cookbook writer, Craig Claiborne, once said something similar to this about a dish in one of his cooking videos. We feel this is perfectly true about this pie!

In the restaurant, we purchased pie shells for ease of baking. At home however, we make our shells from scratch, using a "Foolproof Pie Dough" recipe from Cook's Illustrated magazine. They have a wonderful website filled with tested recipes. We encourage you to find this recipe and use it!

2 ½ Cups Pecans, toasted

3 oz. Dream Chocolate, unsweetened
4 TBSP Butter

4 Eggs, large
1 Cup Corn Syrup
1 Cup Granulated Sugar
¼ tsp Kosher Salt

2 TBSP Espresso Powder
1 TBSP Hot Water

2 TBSP Coffee Liquor, Kamora or Kahlua

Preheat the oven to 300 degrees.

Toast the pecans, either in the oven on a sheet pan or in a skillet over medium heat on the stove. When toasted and cooled, if using Pecan Halves, reserve 3 Tablespoons to use for the top of the pie. The remainder, chop into small pieces. Reserve for later.

Melt the Chocolate and Butter in a small ceramic bowl in the microwave for about 1 minute. Let the mixture cool to 110 degrees before using.

Whisk the Eggs, Corn Syrup, Sugar and Salt together in a medium bowl.

Dissolve the Espresso Powder in the Hot Water and whisk into the Egg mixture.

Add the Coffee Liquor to the Egg mixture.

Add the cooled melted Chocolate and Butter to the Egg mixture and whisk to blend.

Evenly spread the toasted Pecan pieces in the pie shell.

Carefully pour the filling over the Pecans, and then top with the Pecan halves in a design of your choice.

Place in the oven and bake until the filling puffs up and is just set. It will move just a bit. Remove from the oven and cool before cutting.   Yield is 8 pieces.

Reese's Peanut Butter Chocolate Chip Cheesecake

This creamy cheesecake does ask the cook to slow down and follow each step to the letter. The Reese's cups need to be cut into quarter inch pieces and then frozen. The cream cheese is best used at about 68 degrees. Too cold and it clumps, too warm and all the filling falls to the bottom. When whipping it, do so at a low speed, to reduce the air bubbles that will form on the top if beaten too rapidly. It's best to wrap the spring form pan twice with foil, to insure that the water from the water bath stays in the bath. The cheesecake is done when the sides are firm but the center is still a bit jiggly. As soon as possible, after removing the cheesecake from the oven and water bath, remove the foil wrapper and let it cool on a wire rack until it reaches room temperature, then lightly cover with plastic wrap and refrigerate. This is another dessert best made a day ahead of serving! From all these morsels of advice, you all now know the mistakes that were made in our kitchen!

Crust:
5 TBSP Butter, melted and cooled to room temperature
5 oz Graham Crackers (approximately one package), crumbled
⅓ Cup Granulated Sugar
Pinch Table Salt
¼ Cup Cocoa

Filling:
2 Lbs Cream Cheese, at 68 degrees
1 14 oz Can Sweetened Condensed Milk
4 Eggs, at room temperature
1 ½ tsp Vanilla Extract
¾ Cup Chocolate Chips
3 ½ oz Reese's Peanut Butter Cups

Grease a spring form pan and set it aside for use later.

Pre-heat the oven to 300 degrees to bake the crust.

Melt the Butter and set aside to cool.

Place the Graham Crackers, Granulated Sugar, Salt and Cocoa in the bowl of a food processor and process until fine.

Place the crumbs in a small bowl and drizzle the melted Butter into the bowl, using a fork to mix the butter evenly into the crumbs.

When the butter is absorbed evenly, spread the buttered crumbs evenly into the bottom of the spring form pan.

Place a piece of parchment paper over the crumbs and using the a smaller sized round baking pan, press the crumbs into the spring form so that they form a very compressed bottom.

Place on a sheet pan and bake for about 10 minutes.

Remove the crust from the oven and cool. When cool, prepare the pan for filling by wrapping the outside in two layers of foil, tightly enclosing it, so that no water can enter.

Place on a sheet pan and prepare the filling.

Reduce the oven temperature to 275 degrees.

Filling: Use LOW speed for this entire process. Scrape as noted!

Place the Cream Cheese in a mixer bowl and with the paddle attachment, blend until completely smooth. Scrape the sides of the bowl.

Slowly add the Condensed Milk, stopping once in the process to scrape the Cream Cheese from the sides of the bowl.

Add one egg at a time, mixing in thoroughly, stopping the mixer and scraping the sides of the bowl between each egg.

When all eggs are added, add the vanilla, mix until blended.

Remove from the mixer and fold in the Chocolate Chips by hand.

Pour ½ of the batter into the foil wrapped spring form pan.

Sprinkle ½ of the chopped Reese's Peanut Butter Cup pieces over the batter.

Pour in the remaining batter and sprinkle the remainder of the chopped Reese's Peanut Butter Cup pieces on top.
Place the foil wrapped spring form pan in a larger baking pan with at least a 1 ½ inch side.

Place in the oven and fill the baking pan about ½ full with hot water.

Bake for approximately 40 – 50 minutes, until the sides are firm, and the center still a bit jiggly.

Remove from oven when done and as soon as possible, remove the Cheesecake from the water bath, the foil from the pan, and cool on a rack for at least an hour, or until it reaches room temperature.

Cool in the refrigerator covering loosely with plastic wrap.

Yield is 12 pieces.

❧ *The Banana Split Book*

Jeff ordered this book in 2004, the year of 100 year anniversary of the Banana Split. Imagine our surprise when we found our Banana Split listed on page 111! We had no idea! They guessed at the recipe for our Bourbon Walnut sauce, it's close but not exact! Their directions for assembly however, are spot on. A fun read.

News Release   BRICK OVEN BISTRO August 2004

Let's Go Bananas! Dessert celebrates 100 years!
Local Restaurant noted!

In the summer of 1904, a pharmacist from Latrobe, Pennsylvania, took the Ice Cream Sundae to the next level and created the Banana Split. Seldom has one man's taste-making influence paved the way for such a culinary touchstone. It is impossible to imagine an America without the Banana Split. This year's 100th birthday of the Banana Split may have gone unnoticed except for a literary effort by author Michael Turback.
A Month of Sundae's brought him instant recognition as one of the country's leading authorities on ice cream history. Now, in The Banana Split Book: Everything there is to know About America's Greatest Dessert, Turback offers fascinating facts, astounding trivia and fabulous formulas for what he calls the "Liberace of Desserts".

In casting his wide net to collect over 150 versions of the dessert he came to Idaho and visited one of our local restaurant institutions The Brick Oven Bistro! The Bistro Banana Split is featured along with the recipe for the Bourbon Walnut Sauce, one of the sauces on the Bistro dessert.
Celebrate the birthday and the summer, indulge your passions and cool off with a Bistro Banana Split. For the literary, the Banana Split book is available for purchase as well. While you indulge keep in mind that you are helping keep alive an American tradition!

Bistro Shakes and Malts

 From the first day we opened our doors on July 5, 1984, we were known for our hard ice-cream traditional Shakes and Malts. Nearly every staff member, learned how to make our shakes – efficiently! It was all about their "pivot"! Making a shake well was not unlike performing a classic pirouette. The perfect shake was not perfectly smooth, there had to be a lump or two of real ice cream, so you knew you had the real thing!

When we closed our restaurant, our shake station went to Kit's Riverside Restaurant in Horseshoe Bend. Kit promises that he will continue our tradition of delivering delicious old fashioned traditional shakes.

We are including the recipes for some of our more unique combinations! All our shakes and malts were served in traditional shake glasses topped with freshly whipped cream. We made sure there was always an overrun, which we served in a tumbler. Everyone had the choice to share or not.

The directions for these are all the same, blend until nearly, but not completely smooth. To make a shake rather than a malt, leave out the Malt Powder.

Mom's Apple Pie Malt

12 oz French Vanilla Ice Cream
2 Oz Apple Pie Filling
5 Oz Milk
½ tsp Brown Sugar
¼ tsp Cinnamon
2 tsp Malt Powder

Bananas Foster Malt

12 oz French Vanilla Ice Cream
1 Oz Hot Buttered Rum mix (recipe follows)
5 Oz Milk
½ Banana, chopped
2 tsp Malt Powder

Fuzzy Navel Malt

12 oz French Vanilla Ice Cream
2 Oz Fresh Peaches
5 Oz Fresh Squeezed Orange Juice
2 tsp Malt Powder

Pumpkin Pie Malt

12 oz French Vanilla Ice Cream
2 tsp Pumpkin Pie Filling
5 Oz Milk
2 tsp Malt Powder

New York Cheesecake Malt

12 oz French Vanilla Ice Cream
1 Oz Sweet & Sour mix
1 Oz Vanilla Syrup
5 Oz Buttermilk
2 Half pieces of Graham Cracker crushed
2 tsp Malt Powder

Strawberry Cheesecake Malt

12 oz French Vanilla Ice Cream
2 Oz fresh Strawberries
1 Oz Sweet & Sour mix
1 Oz Vanilla Syrup
5 Oz Buttermilk
2 Half pieces of Graham Cracker crushed
2 tsp Malt Powder

251

Wintermint Chocolate Malt

12 oz French Vanilla Ice Cream
1 Oz Chocolate Syrup
¼ tsp Peppermint Extract
5 Oz Milk
2 tsp Malt Powder

Hot Buttered Rum Mix

¼ Lb. Brown Sugar
4 TBSP Butter, softened
pinch Kosher Salt
⅛ tsp Cinnamon
⅛ tsp Cloves, powdered
⅛ tsp Nutmeg

Place all ingredients in a small bowl. Cream butter and remaining ingredients, mixing thoroughly.

And so, we close with the words of our last letter to you in

November, 2012

Dear Boise,

After 28 years, Mom and Dad are flying the coop. You kids are all grown up and it's time you learned to cook for yourselves. We love you and thank you for being such a wonderful family.

Happy cooking and much appreciation, Stephanie & Jeff

253

255

257

259

261

263